HEALING AND HOPE

Michael Hurley SJ

Healing
and Hope

MEMORIES OF AN IRISH ECUMENIST

the columba press

First published in 2003 by
the columba press
55A Spruce Avenue, Stillorgan Industrial Park,
Blackrock, Co Dublin

Cover by Bill Bolger
The cover picture is a detail from *Impression: Sunrise, Le Havre* by
Claude Monet, in the Musée Marmottan, Paris. Used by permission.
Origination by The Columba Press
Printed in Ireland by ColourBooks Ltd, Dublin

ISBN 1 85607 413 7

Contents

For
Cecil McGarry, SJ
and all the many others
who have encouraged me,
especially in my ecumenical vocation,
during these past eighty years
1923-2003

Author's Preface and Acknowledgements

In the first place my appreciation and thanks go to the Heads of Theological Colleges who have so kindly contributed Forewords to this slim volume.

My closest association has been with the Milltown Institute of Theology and Philosophy at Milltown Park in Dublin. I didn't do any of my studies there but I taught areas of systematic theology there from 1958 to 1970. It was during those years that I first became involved in the ecumenical movement and was encouraged to continue my involvement. These were happy and, because of Vatican II, exciting years though not of course without the tensions usual in any lively academic institution. In the 60s one of my students in fact was none other than the Brian Grogan who contributes one of the Forewords. I seem to remember that he was then more attached than I was to the views of the Canadian theologian, Bernard Lonergan. He now presides very successfully over a much larger, more ambitious institution.

Strangely perhaps but Dennis Cooke , President of Edgehill, the Methodist Theological College in Belfast and the contributor of another of the Forewords, I also associate with Milltown Park. I can still see him in our Library where he was a regular reader during the preparation of his doctoral dissertation many years ago. As Minister of Methodist Centenary Church here in Dublin he involved me once in the street preaching which in earlier days was a usual Jesuit ministry and it was he who took the initiative in having me presented as a candidate for an honorary doctorate from the Queen's University of Belfast (QUB). As President of Edgehill Theological College Belfast he has just completed an impressive development of both premises and of programmes. He retires shortly to finish his biography of our mutual friend, Dr Eric Gallagher.

For me The Church of Ireland Theological College here in Dublin will for ever be associated with the day in August 1971 when, as the Divinity Hostel, it hosted a reception for the Black Pope and an international gathering of his cohorts, in other words for the Jesuit General, Fr Pedro Arrupe and the International Congress of Jesuit Ecumenists. Archbishop Buchanan and the Hostel authorities, the late Canon John Brown and the late Canon James Hartin, gave us a warm welcome and a sumptuous luncheon. At any time this would have been an 'act of splendid imprudence', to borrow the words of Owen Chadwick[1] referring to the 1960 visit to the Pope by Archbishop Fisher of Canterbury. It was particularly so at that tense time – internment without trial had just begun in Northern Ireland the previous week. The Theological College, I must add, has, thanks to the present Principal, Adrian Empey who contributes a third Foreword, and to his predecessor, John Bartlett, very kindly given me the opportunity to do some teaching since my return to Dublin in 1993.

Union Theological College, whose Principal also contributes a Foreword, I knew better in the 'old' days when it was called 'Assembly's College'. Patton Taylor I knew before he became Professor and Principal; he was a neighbour on the Antrim Road in Belfast and ready to take communion services for us at times in the Columbanus Community. He now follows in the foot-steps of Principals Haire and Barkley of happy memory whose names feature in the following pages. In those earlier days Assembly's College also had a Matron, Ms Valerie Carson, whose memory is unforgettable. Whenever I came for lunch Valerie would insist on greeting me in the diningroom with a hug, not only to give me a warm welcome but to educate any scandalised students!

My renewed thanks to Adrian, Brian, Dennis and Patton for their generous tributes. They have all my sympathy in their at-tempts to balance the demands of administration and of scholar-ship. I look forward to a greater exchange of students between

---

1. 'The Church of England and the Church of Rome, from the beginning of the nineteenth century to the present day', *Anglican Initiatives in Christian Unity*, ed E. G. W. Bill, SPCK, London 1967, p 101.

the theological colleges of Belfast and Dublin. In principle this could fall within the scope of the Erasmus scheme.

It remains to thank all the others who have helped this book to see the light: Jesuit friends who carefully read the manuscript and made helpful comments: Noel Barber, Brendan Comerford, Eddie FitzGerald, Fergus O'Donoghue and the late Joe Veale who incidentally regretted it recorded more facts than feelings; the librarians: Patricia Quigley (Milltown Park), Slaine O'Hogain (Irish School of Ecumenics) and Raymond Refaussé (Church of Ireland Representative Church Body) who with their staffs have always been outstandingly helpful; Veritas who gave permission to use some materials from Part III (Ecumenical Initiatives) of my *Christian Unity: An Ecumenical Second Spring?*, and Seán O Boyle and his staff at Columba who saw the book through press with their now well-known expertise.

The book is dedicated to all those who have encouraged me down the years in my ecumenical vocation, especially to my fellow-Jesuit, Cecil McGarry SJ. Cecil's service of the whole church and, since 1984, of the church in East Africa in particular, has been quite outstanding. His years of doctoral studies in systematic theology, which were spent at the Gregorian University in Rome, coincided with the early years of the Second Vatican Council (1962-4). Appropriately therefore the interpretation and implementation of Vatican II became his life's work – as theologian, Rector and Provincial here in Ireland and later throughout the whole Jesuit world when in 1975 he was elected as one of four Assistants to our Father General, who was then the famous if controversial Pedro Arrupe. These were difficult, dark days when the Jesuit Order lost the confidence of the Pope, who appointed his own delegate to govern it for two years. When the crisis was happily resolved in 1983, Cecil went to Kenya to continue there his work of implementing Vatican II by teaching and retreat work.[2] I pride myself on the fact that Cecil was one of my own students from 1958 to 1961 and chapters six and seven below allude however briefly to his crucial role in my early ecumenical ministry. In particular, it was he who in that turbulent

2. In 1994 he contributed a chapter (pp 61-79) to the volume on 'Jesuit Journeys in Faith' entitled *Call and Response*, edited by Frances Makower and published by Hodder & Stoughton.

year 1968 secured my reprieve when Archbishop McQuaid wanted me removed from his diocese. To Cecil, therefore, but also to all the others who encouraged me, this volume is dedicated with much appreciation and many thanks.

Finally, I should like to apologise to my Lutheran and Quaker friends who sadly are conspicuous by their absence in this book and to those of my readers who may find the book somewhat repetitive.

Unfortunately the so-called 'main' churches, ie the larger churches, tend to dominate the ecumenical scene in Ireland. I should like therefore to conclude this Preface with some brief Lutheran and Quaker memories. In the summer of 1967 I attended Franklin Sherman's course on Bonhoeffer at the Lutheran School of Theology in Chicago; it was also an immersion course in Lutheranism and its own denominational divisions. In the years 1981-1983 I visited a number of Lutheran religious communities in Germany as part of the feasibility study for the establishment of the Columbanus Community of Reconciliation and was greatly encouraged as well as warmly welcomed. On Reformation Sunday 1999 when in Augsburg the Joint Declaration on the Doctrine of Justification was being formally signed, I had the privilege of giving an address from the pulpit of our Lutheran Church here in Dublin.

I also remember with much appreciation the invaluable con- tribution which Theodore W. Moody, David Poole and Philip Jacob have made to the Irish School of Ecumenics and Rosemary Calvert to the Columbanus Community of Reconciliation, all four being distinguished members of the Religious Society of Friends. But my main Quaker memory is of Victor Bewley's visit to the Jesuit Community at Milltown Park one evening in the late 60s. He began by presiding at our usual evening prayer but in silence in Quaker style, bringing it to an end by shaking hands with me. He then joined us for our evening meal and afterwards gave a talk on Quakerism which I remember chiefly for his an- swer to a question about two-church families. He wasn't enthus- iastic for what seemed a merely practical reason ('there are only twenty four hours in the day') but which in reality revealed a high concept of church membership as involving much more than attendance at Sunday worship.

By its very structure almost, this book involved the risk of repetition. Efforts have been made to reduce the risk and, where some repetition seemed unavoidable, to ensure it was as brief and discreet as possible for the sake of those who read the book from beginning to end, chapter by chapter. But there is little or no logic in the arrangement of the chapters, apart from the first two and the last. So readers can follow the order of their own preferences in deciding how to read the book. Either way I hope they find it an interesting if not also an enjoyable read.

Foreword

by Dennis Cooke

'Céad míle fáilte!' That was the first communication I received from Michael. I was serving as a Methodist minister in Portstewart and had just been appointed to Dublin. I was immediately encouraged by this welcome from a Dublin Jesuit. Previously I felt that I was the one who took the initiative in reaching out to Christians of other communions but here was a priest sending unmistakable signals of Christian friendship before I had even set foot in Dublin! The letter promised an interesting adventure in inter-confessional dialogue and when I met the man himself I was not disappointed. Quite the reverse! My experience of sharing with Michael and observing his work over the years leads me unhesitatingly to dub him the 'Mr Ecumenism' of Ireland.

Michael has excelled in three areas in particular: in offering friendship across the confessional divide; as an ecumenical activist; and, thirdly, as a theologian. I count myself privileged to have been the recipient of Michael's friendship. That first greeting I received in Portstewart was followed by countless other messages, sometimes by letter or card, sometimes by telephone, and often by a personal visit. My guess is that many others have had the same experience!

As an ecumenical activist Michael has no equal. His life is a testament to the fact that goodwill and good ideas must be translated into action. He has carefully fostered many new initiatives in theological thinking and inter-confessional dialogue. The founding of the Irish School of Ecumenics in 1970 was his outstanding achievement. Largely through his vision and careful oversight throughout the first decade of its existence, the contribution this institution has made is immense. The setting up of the International Consultation on Mixed Marriage in September 1973 was significant. On such occasions and others I observed Michael endeavouring to keep on board some of the more conservative minded clergy for whom it must have been a painful experience.

His founding of the Columbanus Community of Reconciliation in 1983 also ranks as one of his many achievements. Members of this community have given unselfish service in Belfast and wider afield during the nineteen years of its existence, not to mention the prayerful ministry exercised daily throughout that period.

Michael has also been a theologian of note. I recall the response from Queen's University of Belfast when they read the lengthy list of his publications and set these alongside the list of his ecumenical initiatives and achievements. There simply was no debate but that he should receive the highest honorary award the university could confer – an Honorary Doctor of Laws. Michael has that rare ability to convey deep theological ideas very simply. For me his best publication has been his most recent, *Christian Unity: an ecumenical spring?* True to his nature he is not afraid to run against official thinking within his communion, evidenced most clearly in the chapter on 'Eucharist: Means and Expression of Unity' in which he skilfully examines the two contrasting schools of thought: is the Eucharist a means of restoring unity between Christians of different traditions? Or is it the expression of unity already restored between Christians of different traditions? He carefully examines the arguments from tradition which supports these positions and then quietly but firmly comes down on the side which suggests there are occasions when the Eucharist can be a means and expression of unity.

These few words very inadequately express the high regard I have for Michael. God sent one of his angels to build bridges across the barriers which Christians had erected between each other – and that angel is Michael Hurley!

Foreword

by Adrian Empey

In one sense this autobiography is superfluous, for the simple reason that there is no shortage of ecumenical achievements for want of which the memory and work of Fr Michael Hurley will fade from the corporate memory of the Christian community in Ireland. That said, its great merit is that they need to be set in the context of the personal record of this modest and self-effacing Jesuit. We have lived through an amazing period of change in the situation of the churches in Ireland during the lifetime of one the primary architects of that change, Michael Hurley. I have no doubt that future generations of historians of the Irish church will turn to this important personal testimony in their efforts to explain that change.

In trying to assess the significance of Michael's chapter entitled 'Anglican Memories', I am mindful of what Trevor Roper once said about history: it is not just the record of what happened, but the record of what happened in the context of what might otherwise have happened. While it is true to say that change would have occurred in Ireland with or without Michael, its actual course owes a great deal to the vision – indeed passion – of this remarkable man. Things do not just happen because they are in some impersonal sense inevitable: the actors are human, and humans are always individual.

Progress in ecumenism needs to be measured from the point of departure. In taking us back to his childhood impressions of the local rural Church of Ireland rector in the 1930s, a somewhat austere bachelor given to writing apologetic works of an unecumenical variety, Michael accurately characterises the situation of the Church of Ireland in the new state. The rector was both courteous and caring in his way, but we are left with an impression of social isolation and a church that was perhaps more at home in a long-departed past than in engaging the present. These impressions are at least echoed in Sheila Chillingworth's article, 'Seventy-five years of Sectarianism', when she recalls life in a Church of Ireland rectory in the 1940s. My own memories of rectory life in the 1950s were much the same. While my father emphatically accepted Irish citizenship, and built up warm relations with the Catholic community, we were never the less conscious that we were a national minority. At the age of 14 I have vivid memories of hundreds of our Catholic neighbours having to stand out of earshot in the graveyard where my father was buried. It was as if we had some sort of religious leprosy. Hope did not exactly come in bucketfuls in such a bleak religious and economic climate. Hope, indeed, usually took the form of emigration.

It is precisely with this background in mind that I read Michael's chapter with such interest and appreciation, for in reaching out the hand of ecumenical friendship he helped to bring a whole community in from the cold. The pages of his chapter are populated with people I know or knew very well, so it is good to see their often courageous part in this remarkable story receiving due recognition. What must be remembered is that none of this was necessarily inevitable, even though it may appear that way in the light of history. It took great courage, profound faith and unshakable commitment to effect the programme of ecumenism in the face of fear, suspicion, and the clinging to a past that really never was what conservatives in both our churches perceived it to be. It is one thing to be a prophet. But prophecies need to be given shape and effect. In so many practical ways – supremely in founding the Irish School of Ecumenics – Michael has ensured that his vision will be carried forward by others.

Nobody believes that we have arrived at the gates of the ecumenical New Jerusalem, but we know that having departed there is no going back. More than that, we rejoice in the memory and goodness of those who pioneered the way. We may also rejoice in the tactical victories that have been won *en route* as well, not least among them the acceptance of the Church of Ireland as part of the wider Christian community on this island, and by extension its place in the future of the nation. Michael has received an honorary doctorate from Trinity College in recognition of his work. What a shame we cannot make him an honorary member of the Church of Ireland as well! Maybe that should be our next ecumenical objective.

Foreword

by Brian Grogan

I began life as a pre-Vatican II anti-ecumenist. Living next door to a Protestant family in a north Dublin suburb, my brother and I waged incessant war on their little daughter, warning her of her impending perdition. The final parting shot in an argument invariably was: 'Well, you're only a Protestant!' On the other hand, my parents used to remark that 'you can't beat a good Protestant'. But dogma won out, and the conviction prevailed in our minds that outside the Roman Catholic Church there was no hope of salvation. I speak of the 1940s when the notion that the Roman Catholic Church could change its mind was simply unthinkable.

I blush as I write the above, but I am also moved with gratitude that I have changed my views. Changes come through interactions between persons, and Michael Hurley stands out as the person who channelled the richness of the decree of Vatican II on ecumenism not only to me but to innumerable others, and not by word alone but by concrete action.

Hailing from Ardmore in County Waterford and educated by the Cistercians in Mount Melleray, Michael joined the Jesuit Order in 1940. On the completion of his basic theological studies in Louvain and his doctorate in Rome, he was assigned to teach theology to Jesuit and Carmelite students at Milltown Park. His early students in the late fifties remember the prodigious energy he brought to this task. For the next forty years he was to labour strenuously to promote the teachings of the Second Vatican Council and especially its teaching on Christian unity and ecumenism. As a student of his in the late sixties, and as his Rector in the seventies, I gradually grew in appreciation of the breadth of vision and consummate daring which he brought to his task.

Work for unity among the churches would need to find incarnate expression in a number of ways. Michael worked at three modes in particular.

Would-be ecumenists need in-depth education to help their respective churches to play an intelligent role in the quest for unity. This called for a centre of ecumenical teaching and research. And so the Irish School of Ecumenics was conceived and brought to birth. Its establishment was a triumph of persuasion and collaboration. As its first Director, 1970-80, Michael not only created and shaped the academic programmes which were to define how the school operated and thought theologically, but developed that spirit of collaboration and learning among staff and students which characterises it still. *Floreat ut pereat* is the motto: May it flourish so richly that it will at some point in the future be no longer needed.

A second mode of incarnating the desire for unity came to Michael during his sabbatical after passing on the directorship to Dr Robin Boyd. Imagine a community of Christians from differing denominations living, working, praying, worshipping together! To many observers, this seemed a pipe dream, but undeterred by cynicism and the prophets of doom, Michael, aided and abetted by others fired by the same vision, established the Columbanus Community of Reconciliation on the Antrim Road in Belfast at the height of the 'Troubles' in 1983. Only those who have dared to build something from nothing can understand all the labour involved. Michael served as Leader for the first ten years, and was familiarly known among his Jesuit friends as the Community's 'abbot'.

Only a few could and did participate in the Columbanus Community: there was need to touch the wider body of Christians and engage them in a practical way in living out their ecumenical task. And so Michael thought up the scheme in the eighties of 'Ecumenical Tithing': one would give one tenth of one's church time or energy to an activity with another church. This project awaits better times.

In his passion for Christian unity Michael has been far ahead of most others in the Roman Catholic Church. Keenly aware of this, and always willing to learn from experience, he sought ways to bring with him people who felt threatened or uncomfortable with his vision and plans. Many conversions occurred: some who were critical of his perceived stances in the seventies had thawed and even become staunch supporters of his ventures in the eighties.

He has known both success and failure. The Irish School of Ecumenics is a wonderful legacy and a gift to the churches. This free-standing ecumenical institute, supported by the main churches, linked academically to Trinity College Dublin, with teaching locations in Dublin and Belfast and a host of evening programmes throughout the country, is the envy of ecumenists in other parts of the world. On the other hand, the recent closure of the Columbanus Community of Reconciliation as a residential community has been a keen disappointment to him.

Michael is a man who does not give up on the big issue, even if failures in detail occur. He is sustained by a high capacity for friendships, of which he has many. They are to be found in all the churches, and are of all ages, female and male, lay and cleric. Within the Jesuit Order he has been a beacon of light and encouragement in matters ecumenical and otherwise to younger Jesuits down the years. His tenacity can be provocative, but fiery arguments with him terminate with no residue of rancour or hurt. He blends zeal with humanity, and with that divine impatience without which many good things would never be accomplished.

Along with people like Austin Flannery, Margaret MacCurtain, Enda McDonagh, Seán Mac Réamoinn, George Otto Simms, Eric Gallagher, Jimmie Haire and a host of others, Michael was part of that ferment in the Irish churches which from the 1960s onwards sought to nudge us all in the direction of a bolder discipleship and a more creative living of the desire of Jesus that all may be one. We are immeasurably in their debt, and the task they laboured at still awaits completion.

Foreword

by J. Patton Taylor

I am pleased to accept this invitation to join with other Theological College Principals in Ireland in writing a foreword for this volume of ecumenical memories by Michael Hurley.

My first contact with Michael was when I was invited to lead occasional devotional services in the Columbanus Community in Belfast. I was impressed with the combination of scholarly learning, deep faith, prayerful devotion, practical concern and commitment to reconciliation and ecumenism which characterised the Community as a whole and Michael as leader. Coming myself from the conservative evangelical tradition of Presbyterianism, I have come to respect those who have demonstrated how much we have in common in the different Christian traditions, while not side-stepping the significance of our differences.

Throughout his ministry, and in particular through the work of the Irish School of Ecumenics, Michael (in his own words) has been in the forefront of 'reconciliation of the people who hold these different doctrinal positions'. This present book speaks volumes of the friendships which Michael has made across the divide, friendships even with those who might have been regarded as 'opponents'. It strikes me that ecumenism that is 'relational' in this way is an essential prerequisite of achieving mutual understanding among Christian traditions.

I am delighted that in his chapter on 'Presbyterian Memories' Michael is able to say: 'Were I to envisage changing my church allegiance, I'd become a Presbyterian'! It is good that the positives of Presbyterianism have been able to shine through the abrasiveness of debate.

In reading through the pages of this volume I have learned a lot about the different traditions Michael describes. Indeed, I have learned a lot about recent Irish Presbyterian history of which I was not aware (being myself a relative newcomer to these shores from Scotland).

I am sure Michael's book will do much to promote the ecumenical reflection and understanding to which he has devoted his life; indeed, the book stands as a tribute to his life's work. I also share his hope that it will bring the reader closer to Jesus and to the gospel faith.

CHAPTER ONE

Introduction

The title of this little volume may be somewhat misleading. For those who are involved in the study of the movement for Christian unity, it will recall the modern emphasis on seeing our goal in the movement as more than merely doctrinal. Ecumenism, many now emphasise, has as its aim and hope not only to reach some common understanding of our differences but also, if not principally, to reach some coming together, some reconciliation of the people who hold these different doctrinal positions. These people have become separated, segregated and estranged because of the differences; their memories, their identities, individual and social, have been shaped by them; their memories therefore need to be healed by a process of contact, conversation and co-operation leading gradually to repentance, forgiveness and reconciliation.

The Irish School of Ecumenics (ISE), especially in the person of Alan D. Falconer – its Director before going to Faith and Order at the World Council of Churches in Geneva – has since the late 80s taken a particular interest in this theme. The first edition of his *Reconciling Memories* was published in 1988.[1] My choice of title does, I hope, owe more than a little to this important, pioneering work but it is also indebted, I think, to my discovery of 'Reminiscence Therapy' during my years in Belfast. This is promoted by, among others, Faith Gibson and the University of Ulster in order to stimulate and energise the elderly, and it is widely used in hospitals and nursing homes.[2] It is also promoted by some spiritual guides in order to help not only the

---

1. Columba Press. The second edition appeared in 1998; in its preparation Joseph Liechy, of the staff of ISE, joined Alan Falconer.
2. I got to know Faith Gibson through her husband, Dr Norman Gibson, who down the years has been a good friend of the ecumenical movement and of the Irish School of Ecumenics and through Margaret

elderly but people of all ages to pray, to arouse in them a spirit of gratitude, of repentance, of forgiveness, of hope. And remembering others is of course the basis for prayer of intercession.

For both of these reasons much of the wall space in my study-bedroom is covered with photographs of people, events and places that have been significant in my life. The photographs lift up my heart: they energise me and help me to pray. It is for both these reasons also that the following pages have been written. Faith Gibson encouraged writers' workshops for the elderly and got the university to set up special courses to teach them how to manage wordprocessing; that scheme was called 'Teaching Older Dogs New Tricks'!

It is sometimes objected that what all of us, especially the churches and especially in Ireland, really need is 'a good dose of amnesia', that it is better to forget than to remember. And indeed 'Acts of Oblivion' as a way of closing a chapter have in fact been a feature not only of secular history but of church history. In 1965 Pope Paul VI and Patriarch Athenagoras I together solemnly consigned to oblivion the excommunications of 1054, 'the memory of which has been, right down to our time, an obstacle to a coming together in charity'. Recent studies, however, seem to agree that in general it is better to remember than to forget, to remember the past so that it never recurs. The influence of the human rights movement is evident in this but, in general and in principle, the aim and hope is not only to obtain justice for past wrongs but also to enable the parties to reach some new *modus vivendi* in peace and harmony. To our great disappointment resistance to Agreed Statements, various forms of sectarianism and general ecumenical apathy have shown only too clearly that, contrary to expectations, bitter memories of the past have not really been forgotten in the churches but only lie hidden waiting to be healed.

We all have unhappy memories and some of mine surface in the following pages. For instance, my failure in the 70s and 80s to maintain good relations with the Catholic hierarchy here in

Wilson, a friend of theirs, who was one of the founder members of the Columbanus Community of Reconciliation. I have also used an article by Sylvia Thompson entitled 'Memories are made of this' which appeared in *The Irish Times* 4 February 1992 p. 9.

Ireland, the failure involved in the recent closing of the
Columbanus Community of Reconciliation. But what matters
surely is how, in what spirit we remember: not wisely but too
well? not trying to see the past steadily and to see it whole but
only partially, in a sectarian spirit? not remembering with the
sweetness and strength of the Spirit (*suaviter sed fortiter*) but with
the bitterness and weakness of our unregenerate selves?

Reminiscence therapy suggests that older people – and I
have now reached the four score – are generally more expert at
coping with any grief and pain which unhappy memories may
cause. Is it that time is a great healer or that with age we become
more open to the healing power of the Spirit? We do know that
the *anamnesis*, the memorial which is the eucharist, depends on
an *epiclesis*, a special invocation of the Spirit. Might it be that in
some analagous way all healing of memories, whether social
and ecclesial in the case of ecumenical activity or individual and
personal in the case of ordinary reminiscence therapy, is dependent on the invocation and presence of the Spirit? Indeed, according to the fourth gospel (Jn 20:19-23) forgiveness is *par excel-
lence* an activity of the Spirit and – more than coincidentally perhaps – the fourth gospel (ibid 14:25, 26) might also allow us to
see the Spirit as the Great Remembrancer for all the followers of
Jesus and not just for the original twelve. It is my hope that the
reminiscing involved in the following pages has been for myself,
and will be for my readers, blessed by the Spirit in whom we remember, repent and forgive, by whom we are healed and filled
with hope.

Hope is, of course, of the essence of the healing of memories
and of any reminiscence therapy. We know from our own experience and that of the human race that success is beyond us here
below; we know from the bible that Christianity is not a religion
of optimism; that it is signed with the sign of the cross, that pain
and suffering and failure remain our lot as they were the lot of
Jesus, 'pioneer and perfecter of our faith' (Heb 12:2) and especially perhaps the lot of those who work to change the structures
of society, religious as well as secular. So I have had to conclude
that there is no cheap hope, as there is no cheap grace; that paradoxically to hope is 'to hope against hope' (cf Rom 4:18) yet with
'the hope that does not disappoint' (cf ibid 5:5).

As a result, I sometimes reason with myself to the effect that the aim of the ecumenical movement is more to promote Christian unity than to establish church union and that, while it is true that the latter is now so remote as to be quite fanciful, the 'stuff as dreams are made on', the former *au contraire* has made extraordinary progress. To adapt the famous or infamous words of Arius in the fourth century: 'there was a time when the movement did not exist'.[3] *A fortiori* there was a time when it did not exist in the Catholic Church. If therefore in these days events are happening which would have been unthinkable even five years ago – for instance Pope John Paul II's remarkable visits in March and May 2001 to Jerusalem and to Athens – then surely other events 'greater than these' will be taking place five and fifty years hence which to us now are equally unthinkable.

This distinction between promoting Christian unity and establishing church union smacks, however, of the distinction between primary and secondary aims. This, for Catholics at least and specially in the theology of marriage, has fallen into disrepute since Vatican II. The two aims of ecumenism are indeed related but not as primary and secondary. This distinction can lead and indeed has led to a demoting of the 'secondary' aim; it can lead to an acquiescence in the *status quo*, to making 'reconciled diversity' an end rather than a means. And I sometimes wonder uneasily if, making physical tiredness an excuse for ecumenical tiredness, I have not just done that in my years of retirement since leaving Belfast in 1993.

Because a boat, a ship is a traditional symbol of the church (as well as of the state), and also probably because the sea is so very much part of my own childhood background, the walls of my study-bedroom display not only personal photographs but also a few prints of ships on the seas of the world. One of the prints is of Paul Henry's 'Launching the Currach'. The seas are rough and it meant a lot to me when in the early 80s we were launching the Columbanus Community of Reconciliation on the stormy seas of Northern Ireland – although it was an embarrassment that all five engaged in Paul Henry's launching were males

---

3. Arius was denying the pre-existence of the Word, the second person of the Trinity, in this simple almost monosyllabic dictum: *en pote hote ouk en*, 'there was a time when the Word did not exist'.

whereas without women the Columbanus Community would never have been launched.

Another print is that of Hokusai's woodcut, 'The Hollow of the Deep Sea Wave off the Coast of Kanagawa'. This was reproduced on the cover of my collection of essays *Christian Unity: An Ecumenical Second Spring?* in 1998. The mountainous waves which Hokusai represents as threatening the Holy Mount Fuji I see as threatening God's kingdom and its values, especially those of unity and peace. It is the boatmen who encourage me: their serenity and the courage with which they ride the waves. One boat shows a Shinto shrine in the stern. All of us, I reflect, but not least ecumenists, must in the power of the Spirit have the Christian courage to go on hoping against hope. We must be 'aglow with the Spirit' if we are to be 'buoyed up by hope' (cf Rom 12:11, 12)

A third of these prints is of the famous painting which, I gather, launched the whole impressionist movement or at least gave it its name: Monet's 'Impression: Soleil Levant'. It gives us the artist's impression of a harbour scene at sunrise, viewed from the window of his studio in Le Havre. The scene suggested is quiet and still: the sun breaking through the morning mists. The background is dark providing glimpses of what look like large vessels, tall masts and perhaps the cranes and gantries I associate with Belfast – all shrouded in mist. The sea, however, is not rough as it is in Paul Henry and Hokusai. It is calm. The few small boats in the foreground are not battling the waves; they lie there idly for the moment but expectantly. The crews have their backs turned to us, their faces to the rising sun, they are waiting for first light, waiting expectantly with one crew member standing in readiness, oar or scull in hand. The orb of the sun is shown making its first appearance and the whole sky is suffused with an orange red glow which is being reflected in the calm waters of the harbour. The light has begun to shine in the darkness but has not yet overcome the darkness.

The quiet and stillness of Monet balance nicely the struggle and stress of Hokusai and of Paul Henry. Can it be true that the mists like the poor we shall always have with us, and that our vocation, especially as ecumenists in the healing of memories, is to wait patiently, in grey areas for the most part , hoping against hope, but with the hope that does not disappoint? The sun must rise? Hope and history must finally rhyme?

To keep on hoping against hope, we need encouragement: encouragement from the life of Jesus himself, especially perhaps as portrayed by Luke, and encouragement from the followers of Jesus, especially in our own day. That is why I humbly and gratefully dedicate this volume of 'memories' to all those who have so generously and faithfully encouraged me in my ecumenical vocation down the years.

CHAPTER TWO

A Jesuit Ecumenical Journey[1]

It all began, or at least the preliminary, preparatory stages of the journey did on 10 May 1923, the date of my birth. As it happened this was the Feast of the Ascension – which means that, because of liturgical revision, I now each year have not only two but three birthdays: 10 May, Ascension Thursday and Ascension Sunday. The Jesuit journey proper began on 10 September 1940 when I entered the noviciate at Emo Park, near Portarlington.

The two places where I spent the intervening years of my youth, at home in Ardmore and at school in Mount Melleray, are both steeped in religion. Ardmore is a little seaside fishing village in Co Waterford on the south coast of Ireland which St Declan hallowed, preaching the gospel there even before St Patrick arrived. Melleray, where I was at school as a boarder from 1935 to 1940, is that bleak mountainside, also in Co Waterford, which has been hallowed for well over a hundred years now by the worship and work of Cistercian monks. Ardmore has a round tower and other early Christian remains and a holy well. Melleray has a monastery. Both are places of devotion and pilgrimage.

My home and family were also deeply religious. It was a religion nourished by a sense of need. The twenties and thirties were difficult times in Ireland. Recovery was slow from the unsettling political and economic effects of the troubles, of the civil war which, having achieved our independence, we fought among ourselves over the terms of the Treaty concluded with the British government. My parents bought and read *The Irish Independent*, they were pro-Treaty in their sympathies. They

1. This chapter incorporates some material from my article 'Triple Vocation' in *Call and Response, Jesuit Journeys in Faith,* ed. Frances Makower, Hodder & Stoughton 1994.

worked hard to make a living for the four of us: my two sisters
(Josie and Eileen), my younger brother (James) and myself. My
mother (Johanna Foley) ran a guesthouse catering for summer
visitors and in this work we all had to give a helping hand. My
father, Martin, started a small business which included selling
petrol and coal and shipping the local fish catches off to the
Billingsgate market in London: periwinkles in the winter,
salmon in spring and lobster in summer. But as a family we remained poor, at least by modern standards. We lived frugally;
going away for summer holidays was out of the question and
without a scholarship I could never have got to secondary
school in Mount Melleray.

This poverty and struggle to make ends meet coloured our
religious sense and deepened our religious commitment. But
our God was no mere God of the gaps on whom we depended
for our temporal as well as our spiritual welfare. Our religion
was much more than a comfort in difficult times: it had a deep
personal quality. God was very real and near, a friend who also
had concerns and strangely needed our help. So there was a
sharing of burdens. Chief among God's concerns were the pagans
abroad and the poor at home. These featured in our life of
prayer and good works. We helped the poor out of our own
poverty, like the widow in the gospels, especially at Christmas
time. We also prayed for and supported the missions. Once, I remember, a family photograph appeared in 'Colm's Corner', a
feature in *The Far East*, a mission magazine which we took as
well as the popular *Messenger of the Sacred Heart*.

But however personal and outgoing, our family religion in
Ardmore was very traditional: it abounded in pious practices
and it aimed to secure for us a safe passage and a safe entry into
heaven after death. We paid visits to the Blessed Sacrament,
made the Stations of the Cross, went to weekly confession and
attended evening devotions – rosary and benediction – on
Sundays and holy days. At home we had Mass celebrated in the
house once a year and every evening we recited the family
rosary, complete with 'trimmings' – additional prayers of intercession led by our mother. In addition I served Mass regularly
and during the summer I would often do so repeatedly because
of the number of priests on holiday saying their private Masses

at side altars. In those pre-Vatican II days each priest was bound to say his individual Mass; a joint celebration round the same altar was out of the question.

As a family we were more religiously active than the average and performed several works 'of supererogation'. These we carried out dutifully even cheerfully, not begrudgingly or resentfully, though not always too devoutly. And we were able to do so not only because of our mother's faith and fervour – our father was less devout – but also because religion in Ardmore in those days was very much a community experience and exercise, shared by the whole village, finding its supreme expression on Sunday mornings and at funerals. Life in a boarding school alongside a Cistercian monastery in the early thirties simply intensified this experience of the corporate as well as personal character of religion in an Irish village some eighty years ago.

So I grew up a pious, innocent and happy youth. At seventeen, in September 1940, I entered the Jesuit noviciate just as the London blitz was beginning. Where did my Jesuit vocation come from? I had won a scholarship to boarding school and in the end I also won a scholarship to university, so despite our family circumstances, a future in some profession would have been open to me. In fact I never thought of a secular career. My experience of organised religion and its ministers, of the church and its priests, both at home and at school, was always positive and good. One of our curates at home became a close family friend and served as my assistant priest when I said my first Mass in 1954. One of the Cistercians in Melleray became a personal friend. My mother's influence was also paramount but she was pushing an already open door. I had always thought of being a priest and my decision, unlike that of my brother (who followed me to the Jesuit noviciate two years later), caused little surprise and no shock. My developing capacity for friendship and the fulfilment I was increasingly finding in friendships must have been an important factor in orientating my thoughts more towards community life in a religious order or congregation than towards the diocesan priesthood. While in Melleray I became enamoured of the Cistercian way of life and what attracted me most was its penitential aspect. Eventually, however, I was led to believe and came to accept that my particular gifts and talents seemed to indicate a calling to the Jesuits rather than the Cistercians, the intellectual apostolate being more prominent among the former than the latter.

My early years as a Jesuit followed what was then the normal pattern for those 'in formation'. Looking back now on this period, what strikes me first is how numerous we were. Twenty-one others joined with me. By the end of the noviceship in 1942 ten had left, but of the remaining twelve only one left later on. Eleven of us were eventually ordained priests and nine of us lived to celebrate our Golden Jubilees in 1990, but only four of us are still alive in 2003.What strikes me, secondly, is that all the houses in which I underwent my formation have ceased to be Jesuit institutions. The noviceship is no longer at Emo Park near Portarlington in the midlands, but has since moved to Dublin and more recently to Birmingham where Irish and British Jesuits now have a joint noviciate. From 1942 to 1945, I lived in Rathfarnham Castle while studying classics at University College Dublin, but Rathfarnham was later sold and young Jesuits studying in Dublin live in Dundrum, Rathmines and elsewhere. From 1945 to 1948, I was in Tullabeg near Tullamore studying philosophy, but Tullabeg was closed some years ago. From Tullabeg I proceeded to Mungret College, Limerick, to teach for three years, but Mungret was closed in the 1970s. From 1951 to 1955, I was in Belgium studying theology at Louvain (where I was ordained priest in August 1954) but that house, too, has ceased to be in Jesuit hands. These facts highlight for me the dramatic changes that have taken place in Jesuit life in my time. In the First World our numbers have fallen sharply but measures are being taken to meet the challenge – new forms of community have been developed as well as new forms of ministry – and elsewhere numbers have begun to grow.

The happiest and probably the most formative of my early years as a Jesuit were those spent in Mungret College from 1948 to 1951. I taught Latin and Irish, supervised the study hall, assisted the headmaster, ran a Mission Society, started a social study circle, trained my senior class to hold a debate in Latin – and managed to avoid having to take games. Opportunities seemed endless and my energies boundless. I came to life and found myself. Two experiences were particularly salutary. One morning after Mass the senior boys, instead of going to the refectory for breakfast, marched rebelliously in the opposite direction out into the grounds to a small recreation room called 'the hut' which they occupied. This hunger strike soon collapsed, but months afterwards I found out that, in the eyes of some of the school authorities, I was being held responsible; that the cause allegedly was the revolutionary Marxist diet the boys were being fed in the social study circle I ran rather than the indifferent food, as they saw it, they were being served in the refectory. I had heard nothing of this allegation until the Provincial came on visitation. I had been condemned unheard. Due process had not been observed and this interpretation of the events, if accepted by the Provincial, could have had very serious repercussions for me. Thanks, however, to the headmaster in whom I confided, the accusation was quashed. Indeed, the paradoxical result was that in the visitation report from the Provincial, special praise was given for the efforts being made in the school, by persons unnamed, to develop the social consciousness of the boys. And instead of postponing my study of theology as a punishment, I was sent on to Louvain. But I had learnt that justice, like charity, must begin at home, that campaigns for justice in Latin America or elsewhere must, to be credible, be accompanied by campaigns for justice at home, not least in the church.

The second experience that stands out in my memory from those Mungret days is more in the area of faith than justice or politics. It emerged that one of our senior boys was not only indifferent and careless about religion but also, despite a physical presence in chapel, was already an unbeliever and an alcoholic. The boy was expelled before too long and in one of his early letters to me he wrote: 'I'm getting on fine without God.' This was 1949 and I was still a theological and spiritual innocent. The blasphemy of the phrase shocked me deeply, cut me to the quick and still haunts me. But it was a salutary if painful experience, especially for someone about to embark on a four-year course in theology. I had learnt that France was not the only European country to be a *pays de mission*.

My working life as a Jesuit falls into four periods: twelve years from 1958 to 1970 teaching systematic theology at Milltown Park in Dublin to the ordinands of the Jesuit and Carmelite

Orders; a decade from 1970 to 1980 also at Milltown Park but now as Director of the Irish School of Ecumenics (ISE) – an inter-church institute for research and postgraduate teaching in the field of ecumenism which I had taken the initiative in founding in Dublin; from 1983 to 1993 as a member of the Columbanus Community of Reconciliation (CCR) which, after a sabbatical year and two years of a feasibility study, I had also taken the initiative in establishing in Belfast; and finally from 1993 until the present in retirement in Dublin.

What I find remarkable on looking back over these forty years and more is the fact that none of it was planned. I certainly didn't choose, I never envisaged a future in theology. What I hoped for was a future in what was until recently The College of Industrial Relations, a Jesuit work. So while in philosophy I made a special study of Marx's *Communist Manifesto*. While in Mungret I organised the social study circle already mentioned and while in Louvain I studied current developments such as Enterprise Councils and spent a good part of my first summer with the Young Christian Workers, getting some experience of what life was like for a Charleroi coalminer, and part of the second summer in the south of France working in a steel factory. It was my superiors who, at the end of my theology, and not until then, assigned me to higher studies with a view to teaching theology.

Neither did I choose ecumenism or envisage, much less plan, a future in interchurch relations. How then did my ecumenical vocation come to develop? It all began in 1959 when the Milltown Park teaching staff decided to hold public lectures. I suggested one on the movement for Christian unity. The suggestion was accepted but, when we searched around for a speaker, we found that there seemed to be no Roman Catholics in the country who had made the subject their own. So I mugged it up myself and the lecture was so timely that I was never allowed to look back. I began to be more and more involved in interchurch relations. This ecumenical work developed side by side with my theology teaching and culminated in 1970 in two events: the commemoration in April of the centenary of the disestablishment of the Church of Ireland for which I edited a volume of essays, and the formal inauguration of the Irish School of Ecumenics in November.

But the intriguing question remains, how in 1959 did I come to suggest ecumenism as a topic for a public lecture when the Second Vatican Council had not yet taken place? Ardmore and my childhood had some part to play. We had our Church of Ireland rector . His congregation even in the summer was small, but still he was in no way ignored in our overwhelmingly Catholic village. It was Louvain, however, which played the principal part in giving my life its ecumenical orientation. Protestants and Orthodox authors featured in our bibliographies. They were open to criticism of course, as were their Catholic counterparts, but their inclusion meant that they were accepted as competent to give authentic, if at times erroneous, interpretations of Christian faith and doctrine; their views were not *ipso facto* suspect, much less proposed for simple refutation. In addition, some of my teachers, especially Pere George Dejaifve SJ, were familiar with and sympathetic to the ecumenical movement. While I was in Rome doing doctoral work from 1956 to 1958, my rector was the ecumenical pioneer, Charles Boyer SJ, whose Foyer Unitas sponsored lectures which I sometimes attended. I should also note that the bishop who ordained me on 15 August 1954 was none other than Leon-Joseph Suenens who was to become one of the great influential personalities of Vatican II and who then, as Auxiliary Bishop of Malines, was fully conscious of the ecumenical tradition he was inheriting and was already aspiring to be a worthy successor to Cardinal Mercier.

Looking back now on these forty and more years, I am amazed to see how much change was happening in my life. New horizons, new worlds were opening up for me. I was taking my first steps in interchurch relations, being introduced to Anglicanism and Methodism and Presbyterianism, and gradually coming to feel I belonged. In the second place, speaking engagements at home and abroad were multiplying and providing opportunities for travel, so I was privileged to lecture in Rome and Reykjavik, Ottawa and New Orleans, Melbourne and Minneapolis as well as in Maynooth and the Presbyterian Theological College in Belfast. In the third place, there were new ventures in the beginnings of which I was very much involved: the Milltown Park public lectures, the annual Glenstal ecumenical

conference, the annual Greenhills ecumenical conference, the
Irish Theological Association, the International Congress of
Jesuit Ecumenists, the Irish School of Ecumenics, the World
Methodist Council-Roman Catholic Church International Com-
mission and, finally, the Columbanus Community of Reconcil-
iation.

In retrospect, the sixties and seventies were certainly exciting. But they brought various tensions: tensions with students
and with colleagues about, for instance, Bernard Lonergan's
theology, about pluralism in theology and about a preferential
option for the poor; tensions with censors and superiors about
views expressed in articles intended for publication and submitted, according to Jesuit custom, for prior approval; and tensions
with the Catholic hierarchy, especially in the context of the
International Consultation on Mixed Marriage held in 1974
which led to strained relations with the Episcopal Commission
on Ecumenism and with the Catholic Archbishop of Dublin.
With hindsight I can now see how much tensions within myself
(my own inadequacies and insensitivities and indiscretions)
were a complicating factor in all these situations. But I managed
to survive. I survived because I am blessed with the precious
gifts of perseverance and resilience; because at critical moments
encouragement was always forthcoming from one source or another; but above all because a number of young Jesuit students,
initiating an experiment in small group living at Milltown Park
in the early seventies, invited me to join them in what came to be
called the Basement Community. This community turned out to
be a notable success. I was an ordinary member. I did act as a
sort of resident chaplain who presided at the eucharist, but
otherwise I had no authority. The group, however, provided me
with the congenial company and support which enabled me to
live happily as a Jesuit and an ecumenist.

When I retired as Director of the Irish School of Ecumenics in
1980 the idea was that the School, already ten years old, could
begin to find its own feet without me and that after a sabbatical I
would offer my services to a seminary or theological college in
Africa for a period of years. The sabbatical was a gloriously exhilarating experience which confirmed and renewed me in my
Jesuit and ecumenical vocations, not least the Jesuit one, and set

me off in an altogether unexpected direction. I was breaking fresh ground both geographically and ecumenically as I travelled in Greece and the Holy Land, in Africa and India and got into China to what was the end of the medieval silk route at Xian and further on to Beijing.

This was my first real experience of the other world religions and it left me with challenging, indeed disturbing questions, especially about Islam which, I then felt, should not have been able to conquer Christianity in places like Egypt and to forestall it in places like north India. But it was my Jesuit vocation which, I think, benefited most from the sabbatical. A Jesuit, I discovered in a new way during the year, is someone who is fortunate enough to have a home from home all over the world. He belongs to a far-flung company of men who, like the rest, are sinners but who, at their best, are generous, bold and imaginative in their devotion to and service of Christ and the gospel. I never before felt so grateful for, so proud indeed, of my Jesuit vocation as when I attended Mass at the Tan Tang, the seventeenth-century Jesuit church in Beijing, and prayed at the tombs of the pioneering Jesuits Ricci, Verbiest and Schall, and visited Agra and Fatehpur Sikri where in the sixteenth century the Mogul Emperor, Akbar, had Jesuits at his court; or when I stayed with Jesuits in such a variety of places as the island of Syros, Addis Ababa, Varanasi, Kathmandu and, of course, Zambia and Hong Kong where Irish Jesuits, my own brother included, have laboured and continue to labour so devotedly.

The main result of my sabbatical (1980-1) was again something unplanned: the Columbanus Community of Reconciliation (CCR). Instead of teaching theology in Port Harcourt or Nairobi or some place else in Africa as envisaged originally, I became involved in helping to get an interchurch residential community established in Belfast. The idea came into my head in the middle of a thirty-day retreat which I was doing in the little Indian village of Sitagarha near Hazaribagh in north-east India. It had been in my mind in 1969, as is clear from the last chapter and last page of *Irish Anglicanism*, but it had disappeared from my consciousness during the seventies and emerged as a completely new suggestion in February 1981. An attempt, however, by a religious to start some sort of an interdenominational residential community can only seem entirely logical if one of the basic insights of the ecumenical movement is that the churches should do everything together as far as conscience permits. For an ecumenist, too, it could only seem entirely logical to feel called to undertake such an initiative in a place where the scandal of Christian disunity is particularly grave. After the retreat, therefore, the idea grew on me and seemed good to some, though not to all, of the Jesuit friends whom I consulted. In particular it commended itself to my Provincial Superior.On my return home in the summer of 1981 he suggested that I carry out a feasibility study.

The moment could hardly have been more inauspicious. The feasibility study happened, unfortunately, to coincide with the most difficult and tense years in the whole tempestuous history of the Jesuits. Relations between the Society of Jesus and the papacy reached an all-time low in 1981 when the Pope intervened in the normal procedures of Jesuit government and nominated a delegate of his own to govern the Society. Reactions varied: there was much support and sympathy but also much embarrassment and confusion as well as indignation and anger among Jesuits. Happily, before too long communication and confidence were restored and the storm blew over. But while it lasted was hardly the most propitious moment for a Jesuit to get involved in, much less take a leading part in, a new and ecumenical initiative. But despite the general nervousness of the times, my superiors, so far from discouraging me or in an excess of caution suggesting that I postpone the venture for the moment, gave me their full support, insisting only that I proceed with the utmost care and correctness.

So it was that early on I sought and secured interviews with Cardinal Ó Fiaich, with two members of the Episcopal Commission on Ecumenism (Bishop Cahal Daly then in Longford, and the late Bishop Kevin McNamara then in Kerry), with the President of the Vatican Unity Secretariat (as it was then called) Cardinal Wiliebrands and with the Vice-President, Bishop Torrelia. The reaction of all five was quite positive though understandably guarded and cautionary on the question of eucharistic sharing. The reaction of the other churches was also positive and, in due course, the Columbanus Community was formally inaugurated at 683 Antrim Road in Belfast on 23 November 1983. This was the feast day of St Columbanus, the younger contemporary of Columba of Derry and Iona, who has been called Ireland's first European because he went from Bangor, Co Down, to establish communities at Luxeuil in France and at Bobbio in Italy. He died in 615.

This third period of my Jesuit working life from 1983 to 1993 was unexpectedly rewarding and happy. For me personally it meant a resumption of my involvement in the life and work of the Irish School of Ecumenics. Each of us in the Columbanus Community sought outside work of some sort. So when the ISE part-time post of Lecturer in Continuing Education, a post based in Northern Ireland, became vacant, I applied and was appointed. This put me in charge of ISE activities in Northern Ireland, in particular of the Certificate course we ran in Derry and Belfast in association with the University of Ulster. None of us in the Columbanus Community had any illusions that we would solve the Northern Ireland problem. Our main aim was to give encouragement to those who were committed to improving community relations and to do so more by deed than by word: by giving an example of integrated living in an increasingly segregated city. Many confirmed us in believing that in our modest way we were an encouraging sign of hope. But after ten years I decided to retire for the same reason as I retired from the School of Ecumenics: to enable CCR to find its own feet. I retired back to Dublin to the Milltown Park Jesuit Community in September 1993.

It was very satisfying for me personally that my last two years in Belfast, in ISE and CCR, were spent directing a research project on 'Reconciliation in Religion and Society', that we were able to present the findings in a residential seminar in Belfast in early May 1993 and that the findings were published the following year by the Institute of Irish Studies at QUB. From Milltown Park as my base, I continue to reflect and write on the nature of reconciliation and the role of forgiveness. This is the theme which has dominated my public speaking and writing since returning to Dublin. In October 1994 in the aftermath of the cease-fires I took the liberty, in a letter to individual church leaders and to some of the religious press, of suggesting that 'we in the church should be more zealous than ever and more imaginative than ever in exercising our ministry of forgiveness'. In April 1996 'Hope and Forgiveness' was my theme when invited to preach in the chapel of King's College, Cambridge. The collection of my articles which appeared in 1998 under the title *Christian Unity: An Ecumenical Second Spring?* included one chapter on 'Reconciliaton and Forgiveness'. In October 2002 'The Ecumenical Methodology of Forgiveness' was the title of a paper which I prepared and read for a group of European Jesuits meeting at Velehrad in the Czech Republic to discuss the role of Jesuits in East/West interchurch relations. My ecumenical activity is now limited, but I have introduced in the Jesuit community here the custom of inviting someone from another church to take supper with us and then preside at evening prayer on a few occasions during the annual January Unity Week. This is a simple application of my principle that ecumenism should as far as possible not be an additional activity but an ordinary one done for a change on an interchurch or some other ecumenical basis.

It is now forty five years since I was first appointed to be a member of this Milltown Park Jesuit community. During my ten years in Belfast I remained formally a member and was happy to dedicate the collection just mentioned 'to the Jesuit Community at Milltown Park in gratitude for forty years of membership'. I look forward to ending my days here.

CHAPTER THREE

Anglican Memories

My home village of Ardmore, Co Waterford had, as mentioned in the previous chapter, its own Church of Ireland church and rector, so my first introduction to Anglicans happened I was a young boy in the 1930s, in those pre-Vatican II days when for the most part Catholics and Protestants, like the Jews and Samaritans of old, 'had no dealings with each other'. It wasn't altogether a happy introduction. Because Ardmore, a seaside village, was then a summer resort for some of the Blackwater Valley gentry, most of the Anglicans I came to know, however slightly and from a distance, bore more resemblance to Molly Keane's characters in her novels than to those of Sean O'Casey in his plays, little resemblance to the people of the Shankill in Belfast.

The church in Ardmore, a pre-Patrician church founded by St Declan, was then in the diocese of Waterford and Lismore but recently – with more regard for convenience than for history – it has been transferred to the diocese of Cork by the Church of Ireland authorities. Our rector I remember as a tall, gaunt, somewhat forbidding bachelor. It was a surprise to discover later on that he was the author of a book which, not untypically of course for the time, was of a controversial, unecumenical character, unsympathetic to Roman Catholics.[1] It came as a surprise because, though I remember him as a somewhat forbidding character, I often saw my father and himself chatting around the village and, when one of my aunts was unwell, he is reported to have called to make enquiries about her health – unlike (it was duly noted) either of his Catholic counterparts. My surprise was of

1. J.Warren, *Ireland and her Fairy Godmother*, 2nd ed. Dublin, Corrigan & Wilson, 13 Sackville Place, 1909. He was also the author of one other book and a number of pamphlets, most of which I have been able to see thanks to the courtesy of Dr Raymond Refaussé, Librarian and Archivist of the Representative Church Body Library.

course naïve: controversial thinking and charitable living can go hand in hand.

My next significant encounter with Anglicans was not until March 1960. In between I had become a Jesuit and had studied theology in Louvain (1951-5). Here I found that our reading lists included Anglican, Lutheran and Orthodox authors as well as Catholic and that all were open to criticism, Catholics included. In retrospect, I see this as a significant acknowledgement that Anglicans and others are, like Catholics, authentic, if at times erroneous, interpreters of the Christian revelation. One of our teachers had a particular interest in ecumenism and had visited Orthodox monasteries in Greece and Anglican religious communities in England. Every January we celebrated the Week of Prayer for Christian Unity. And when I moved to Rome for postgraduate work (1956-8) my rector was Charles Boyer SJ, who was director of an Ecumenical Centre where I attended a lecture on the ecumenical movement given by the great Bishop Bell very shortly before he died.

It was on 9 March 1960 that my own ecumenical ministry began. I was teaching systematic theology at Milltown Park in Dublin and that was the date on which a public lecture on 'The Ecumenical Movement' was given there, with myself as the speaker. The lecture was welcomed especially by those interested in ecumenism who realised that pan-Protestantism, for all its merits, was no real answer to the ecumenical problem. These were mostly but not exclusively Anglicans, and foremost among them was Raymond Jenkins, then Archdeacon of Dublin who took me under his wing and proceeded to give me the sort of practical introduction to Anglicanism that led me in due course to make 'fieldwork' a required component in the programmes of the Irish School of Ecumenics.

My first major ecumenical invitation I owe to Professor F.E. Vokes, then Archbishop King Professor of Divinity at Trinity College, Dublin (TCD) who was also President of the TCD branch of the Student Christian Movement (SCM). The Second Vatican Council had been summoned and in May 1962 (before the Council opened) I was invited to address the branch on 'The Vatican Council and the Ecumenical Situation Today'. It was my first major ecumenical invitation and it was my first experience of the difficulties to be experienced by a Catholic ecumenist. According to the Catholic Archbishop of Dublin, Dr J. C. McQuaid, TCD was forbidden territory for Catholics and my Jesuit superiors took a strict view of the Archbishop's wishes and so I had to decline the invitation. But Professor Vokes and the SCM saw a way of circumventing the obstacle. For my sake, the meeting would be held outside the walls, off campus. The venue was transferred to the Cumberland Hotel in Westland Row, so I was free to accept the invitation. Thankfully the attitudes which led to these manoeuvrings have disappeared and so also, symbolically perhaps, the Cumberland Hotel in which the SCM meeting took place, and the journal in which my paper was published later that same year, *The Irish Ecclesiastical Record* (July 1962).

My next ecumenical adventure was in the Church of Ireland chaplaincy of the Queen's University of Belfast (QUB) in mid October 1962 at the invitation of Maurice Carey, then chaplain. This time there was no need for any manoeuvrings. The text of my Milltown Park public lecture had been published as a pamphlet by Veritas in January of 1961. It was entitled *Towards Christian Unity* and Bishop Mageean, Bishop of Down and Connor had sent me a personal letter of thanks, and in his Lenten pastoral letter to his clergy and people that year had written: 'I cordially commend it to you to read and study'. In some ways, at least, Belfast was clearly more ecumenical than Dublin and when I approached the Catholic chaplain at QUB about the invitation from Maurice, his Church of Ireland colleague, he invited me to stay with him at the Catholic chaplaincy for the weekend and to preside and preach at the Catholic students' Sunday Mass in Aquinas Hall.

That Belfast weekend was memorable for many reasons. It was my first visit to Northern Ireland and Maurice, who met me off the train, showed me some of the Belfast sights, especially the dominant, domineering edifice of Stormont. And as we drove around he was also gently reminding me that, if Anglicans were Protestants, they were Protestants with a big difference. I was very glad to have been able to preach for Maurice at St John's Sandymount in Dublin shortly before he died. That weekend in Belfast also marked the opening of Vatican II and its ecumenical possibilities were, of course, the theme of my homily and of my

talk. Among the personalities I met over the weekend were Fr
Cahal Daly, then lecturer in philosophy at Queen's, now
Cardinal, who came to lunch at the Catholic chaplaincy on the
Sunday, Principal J. L. M. Haire whose guest I was to lunch at
the Presbyterian Theological College, and Professor J. C. Beckett
whose guests for supper Maurice and I were before the meeting
at the Church of Ireland chaplaincy on the Sunday evening. I remember that meeting as more lively and controversial than the
SCM meeting in Dublin. Some of the students were preoccupied
with papal infallibility

All during the 60s and indeed right up to his death in 1998
Archdeacon Jenkins continued to act as my tutor in Anglicanism.
He introduced me not only to the life of his own parish of All
Saints, Grangegorman, and to one of its most famous parish-
ioners, George Tyrrell who later became a Jesuit but died an ex-
Jesuit , a casualty of the modernist crisis. He also introduced me
to many others, especially to Tom Salmon, Dean of Christ
Church – who used to keep a special seat for me in the sanctuary
on special occasions – and indeed to the whole life of the
Anglican Church by, for instance, lending me biographies of
some of its distinguished leaders.

One of my most cherished memories is of the meeting of
'Ham and Eggs', a Church of Ireland clerical society which,
thanks to the archdeacon, I attended as a guest and addressed at
his vicarage on the morning of 10 February 1964. I remember in
particular kneeling with him and the other eleven members of
this society or breakfast club, and sharing their devotions and
making the embarrassing discovery that Anglicans – and other
Christians likewise – were not only people with different doc-
trines and ways of worship but also people who like us 'said
their prayers'. The devotion I experienced that morning was
something I had never before experienced and – scandalous to
admit – never before knew or thought to exist outside my own
church. Another particular memory of that morning is of Dean
Emerson of Christ Church who had written to me in advance
and given me the text of the question he hoped to ask in the discussion after my paper. This was not just simple courtesy. More
significantly it was for me a clear sign that the age of controversy
and winning theological debates was over, that the new age of

ecumenism had really dawned: now the churches were together searching for the truth so that the world might believe.

1966 I remember as the year I published an article in *The Furrow* entitled 'Non Anglicani sed Angli?' and subsequently got a letter of reprimand from Lambeth Palace. In November of that year it had been announced that an Anglican/Roman Catholic Joint Preparatory Commission had been established. My article criticised the Anglican membership of this Commission on three grounds. The third was the absence of a member of the Church of Ireland. I was merely supporting my friend Andy Willis, editor of the *Church of Ireland Gazette* who had written a critical editorial in his issue of 11 November and who reprinted my article in January. Lambeth Palace, however, was aggrieved and annoyed. For their part, the Anglican authorities had in fact wanted to include Bishop McAdoo as a member and therefore felt that they didn't deserve criticism or blame. It was apparently the Church of Ireland which had objected, probably in the person of the Primate Archbishop McCann. Lambeth felt that we should have known all this. Happily Bishop McAdoo did become a member of that Preparatory Commission after its first meeting and went on to be co-Chairman of its successor body the Anglican/Roman Catholic International Commission.

My next encounter with Anglicanism was the volume of essays I edited on the occasion of the centenary of disestablishment in 1970. In the years immediately preceding, various other significant encounters took place among which the following stand out in my memory. *Praying for Unity* appeared in December 1963 with an Introductory Message from Archbishop George Simms, then in Dublin, as well as from the other church leaders and was well received. The West Cork Clerical Society invited me to be their main speaker at a widely-publicised meeting in Kenmare in March 1964. That June the first Glenstal Ecumenical Conference was held with strong Anglican support from, among others, the Dean of St Patrick's in Dublin, John Armstrong, the Dean of Ardfert, Charles Gray-Stack and the Rector of St George's in Belfast, Edgar Turner, all three of whom were speakers. In June of 1965 I published a comment on 'The Five Per Cent', a series of *Irish Times* articles by Michael Viney on Protestantism in the Republic. My comment which appeared in

The Furrow was reprinted by the *Irish Times* and became the subject of a long and laudatory editorial in *The Church of Ireland
Gazette* on 9 July. With typical generosity Canon Willis wrote
that 'it has taken a Jesuit priest to make the most comprehensive
and critically constructive assessment of the recent *Irish Times*
articles'. In January 1966 during Unity Week, the first Greenhills
Ecumenical Conference took place but only after John Armstrong
and Archbishop George Simms had succeeded in overcoming
the initial reluctance of Archbishop McCann of Armagh in
whose diocese Greenhills was located. One of the two main
speakers was the Dean of Cork, Eric Daunt. As with the Glenstal
so with the Greenhills Conference, I was a member of the organising committee and remained so for many years.

In 1967 I was away for the first half of the year teaching in
Ottawa and then in the latter part busy, among other things,
preparing my edition of John Wesley's *Letter to a Roman Catholic*.
It was in the summer of the following year 1968 that the idea
first came to my mind of an interdenominational volume of essays to present to the Church of Ireland in 1970 on the occasion
of the centenary of disestablishment. The eventual publication
and formal presentation of this book marked a turning point in
my ecumenical life and significantly, perhaps, it all happened on
15 April 1970, just a decade after my very first ecumenical engagement (my Milltown Park Public Lecture on 9 March 1960).
15 April 1970 marked a turning point for me because the wide
support and warm welcome which *Irish Anglicanism (1869-1969)*
received went a great way towards ensuring that the two major
projects which I was subsequently to undertake (the Irish School
of Ecumenics and the Columbanus Community of Reconciliation) were also received positively.

The story of the disestablishment book I have already told in
the Spring 1995 issue of *Search*. It only remains here to stress that
the book is really a monument to the late Allen Figgis, not only
to his expertise as a publisher but also to his love for the Church
of Ireland and to his remarkable gift as an encourager. In the
early days, when there was no promise of a government grant to
make the project financially viable, he was the only publisher to
take an interest in the project. I add two particular memories.
The first is of a phone call from Mrs Simms, wife of the

Archbishop whom I knew as a regular attender at the Milltown Park Public Lectures, as someone who always rose to defend Archbishop McQuaid whenever he was criticised. Mrs Simms rang to ask if I could possibly find out for her what sort of dress the Taoiseach's wife, Mrs Lynch, would be wearing at the presentation ceremonies which would begin with a church service, be followed by a reception and end with a dinner party. Very characteristically she didn't want to be different and possibly be thought to be upstaging Mrs Lynch. Being naturally out of my depth, I was only too happy to hand that question over to the Taoiseach's private secretary. The second memory is of the embarrassment of the ushers, all Jesuit students, when in the dining room the bishops introduced themselves by giving the name of their See rather than their surname and of my embarrassment at not having provided both.

One of the photographs which I treasure is of John Armstrong, then Bishop of Waterford and Lismore, Anthony Hanson, Head of the Department of Theology at the University of Hull, Sir Brynmor Jones, Vice-Chancellor of the University and myself. We're all in jovial mood and one reason is not too far to seek. The date is 16 July 1971, the occasion is a press conference to announce that, beginning in the Autumn, duly qualified students of the Irish School of Ecumenics will be eligible for the postgraduate degree of B.Phil from the University of Hull; the location is the Gresham Hotel, Dublin who hosted the occasion.

1970 had been a *longus et unus annus*, very much an eventful year. The celebrations of 15 April were followed on 28 May by a press conference announcing the establishment of the Irish School of Ecumenics (ISE) with Bishop John Armstrong present as its Anglican Patron; by a hectic summer in which I sought support from among others, Principal John Hapgood of Queen's College, Birmingham (later to be Archbishop of York) and from Professor Gordon Dunstan of King's College London and editor of *Theology*, who agreed to carry an insert in a forthcoming issue; and by the formal inauguration of ISE on 9 November by the General Secretary of the World Council of Churches, Rev Dr Eugene Carson Blake, in the presence of a large gathering of church people and academics.

ISE, however, had begun that Autumn but without any academic accreditation for its courses. Our hope had been in Trinity College, Dublin (TCD) but when they showed no real interest I remembered a visit from Anthony Hanson during the summer when he offered help from Hull. It was entirely due to Anthony's influence and efforts on our behalf that the Vice-Chancellor of the University was able to fly in on 16 July the following year and make the happy announcement that Hull University would act as our accrediting agency. ISE owes an immense debt to Anthony Hanson and for that reason I was more than happy to have been invited to give the address at the memorial service for him in Thirsk in Yorkshire on 18 September 1991.[2]

1971 is also memorable for me because the International Congress of Jesuit Ecumenists met in Dublin and was addressed by our General, Fr Pedro Arrupe. Some of the 120 participants were housed by local clergy, including the rectors of Sandford and Donnybrook and were greatly impressed by their hospitality. But what impressed the Jesuits most of all perhaps was the speech at the opening dinner by The Tánaiste, Mr Erskine Childers, and the luncheon provided for them by Archbishop Buchanan and the Church of Ireland Divinity Hostel. The Congress was taking place in mid August and that month the political situation in Northern Ireland was extremely tense. On 9 August internment without trial had begun but the series of dawn raids by the army to arrest hundreds of suspected IRA members had left 22 people killed (including one Catholic priest) and 7000 homeless. Violence only increased during the rest of the year and the following January was to see the events of Bloody Sunday. In that tense atmosphere the generous words of Mr Childers were deeply moving; he told the story of his father shaking hands with the firing squad who executed him during the Civil War in 1922 and speaking of 'this horror of the war of brothers'; in the very much worse situation of 1971 Mr Childers urged restraint and ecumenical tolerance and under-standing instead of bigotry and hate.

Archbishop Alan Buchanan, as a Northener who had just been bishop of the cross border diocese of Clogher, knew at first hand what the politico-religious situation was like in the North.

---

2. For an account of the beginnings of ISE cf my essay in *Christian Unity: An Ecumenical Second Spring?* Dublin 1998, pp 265-291, 388-393.

He was also fully aware of the attacks already under way in Northern Ireland against ecumenism in general and the World Council of Churches (WCC) in particular. WCC, it was alleged, was promoting 'a Romeward trend in Protestanism' and supporting terrorists in Africa if not in Northern Ireland. Under those circumstances, and because Jesuits are the particular *bêtes noires* of Dr Ian Paisley and those who oppose ecumenism, it was immensely courageous and magnanimous of the Church of Ireland to entertain to lunch at the Divinity Hostel a large international group of us including our Father General, and to give us such a warm welcome.

The International Consultation on Mixed Marriage which took place from 2-4 September 1974 was probably the most ambitious project of the Irish School of Ecumenics during my ten years as Director. It was also a project which the Church of Ireland greatly welcomed. The School's relationship with Anglicans had in the meantime developed. Two of its principal supporters were Mr Fred Combe of Dublin, who became a Trustee of ISE, and Commander Claud Herdman of Sion Mills, both of them evangelicals. One of ISE's very first students (Rev Austin Masters) went on to become Assistant Secretary of the Missionary and Ecumenical Council of the General Synod of the Church of England. Bishops Richard Hanson and Henry McAdoo became members of the Academic Council and helped with teaching. Bishop Hanson greatly appreciated these occasional brief respites from what he found to be the unecumenical realities of his Clogher diocese. On St Patrick's Day 1972, thanks to Dean Victor Griffin, I preached in St Patrick's Cathedral, Dublin (a special service against the background of Bloody Sunday) and on 22 October at the Harvest Thanksgiving in All Saints, Mullingar. On 17 November I gave the address at the annual King's Hospital Prizegiving and in Unity Week 1973 Canon Malcolm Graham, undaunted by the prospect of an Orange protest, bravely invited me to preach in his Church of Ireland church at Rostrevor – all these historical firsts apparently. And on 20 July 1973, on the occasion of the Dublin meeting of the Anglican Consultative Council, a number of Anglican dignitaries, including the Archbishop of Canterbury, Michael Ramsey, accepted invitations to a luncheon hosted by the School.

The Anglican contribution to the International Consultation on Mixed Marriage was outstanding. It was made firstly by Bishop Kenneth Cragg, the expert on Islam, who read a paper on 'A Christian-Muslim Perspective' and who by his paper did much to persuade the School to include an Interfaith Relations section in its academic programme. Secondly by Professor Gordon Dunstan of King's College London, who was a member of the Anglican/Roman Catholic Commission on Marriage and Mixed Marriage and whose paper anticipated some of the conclusions of that Commission. Professor Dunstan unfortunately took ill during the Consultation. Afterwards he was instrumental in establishing the School's London Lecture which for many years took place annually around St Patrick's Day at King's College.Thirdly by Canon Martin Reardon and his Catholic wife Ruth who took part in a symposium on 'Living an Interchurch Marriage'. Fourthly by Archbishop Simms who, as the finale of the Consultation, presided at a celebration of the eucharist in the community chapel at Milltown Park. A number of speeches at General Synod the following June made very kind references to the School and its 'dynamic and enthusiastic Director' and to the Consultation. The Consultation, however, was as unwelcome to our Catholic bishops as it was welcome to the Church of Ireland.

When the idea of what eventually became the Columbanus Community of Reconciliation came to me out of the blue on 18 February 1981, it came to me in a place in India which has close ties with the Church of Ireland. I was on retreat in Sitagarha and when cycling around I met individuals who had become Christian through the work of the Dublin University Mission to Chota Nagpur. I also visited St Columba's College and St Columba's Hospital in Hazaribagh founded by the Mission; at the hospital I was welcomed by Dr Maureen Murphy. The previous month I had visited the Brotherhood of the Ascended Christ in Delhi established by the Cambridge Mission and later I visited the Oxford Mission near Calcutta. Whether these Anglican initiatives influenced me I don't know but Anglican support for CCR, when in due course it became a project and a reality, was considerable and of course crucial for what was envisaged as an interdenominational venture.

By this time John Armstrong was in Armagh as Primate. He

was as ever encouraging and became Anglican Patron of the Columbanus Community. Encouraging also were Bishop Mc Cappin and Bishop (now Archbishop) Eames, both with jurisdiction in Belfast where we wanted to be located. Two of their clergy, Canon Edgar Turner and Canon Hammie Leckey, became Anglican Sponsors of the project. We eventually got a house at 683 Antrim Road and the local rector and his wife, the late Will and Margaret Harris, could not have been more welcoming and helpful.

The Church of England Advisory Council for Religious Communities was also particularly encouraging. I visited a number of them and one of the founding members of CCR was Sister Eileen Mary of the Sisters of the Love of God in Oxford. Subsequently three other Anglican religious became members: Sisters Elspeth and Marion of the Order of the Holy Paraclete in Whitby and Sister Louise of the Community of St Mary the Virgin in Oxford. I shall always remember my first meeting with Sr Eileen Mary – at Farm St in London. I did my best to hide my shock at her voluminous habit but she and her community had no difficulty in accepting that secular dress would be more appropriate in CCR in order not to scandalise Protestant Belfast.

Looking back on my ten year stint in Belfast in the Columbanus Community, and remembering the support I received from Church of Ireland friends, I recall with sadness that three of them have already passed on. There was Chuck McClenaghan who had been a student at ISE in Dublin but whose home was in Donegal at Rathmullan, where I was always welcome especially when on my way to Derry for study weekends. There was Sylvia Kastell who did the ISE Certificate course in Belfast and who became a faithful supporter of all CCR activities, and Doreen Freer also an ISE student who became Honorary Secretary of the CCR project during the two preparatory years (1981-3). Doreen, a former teacher, spoke for all three and others when she once greeted me with a clever play on the motto of ISE: *floreat ut pereat*, 'may it flourish in order to perish'. She wrote: *floreas ne pereamus*, 'may you flourish lest we perish'. I had no difficulty in reciprocating: *floreas ne peream*, 'may you flourish lest I perish'. I feel these three, and all my other friends who have passed away, still console and support me with their prayers from above.

CCR was privileged to receive quite a number of distinguished visitors. Perhaps the most distinguished Anglican visitor
in my time was George Carey who retired last year as Archbishop
of Canterbury. In May 1988 after lecturing in Corrymeela he came
to CCR, addressed a small group of members and invited guests
for what we used to call a 'Vision Evening', stayed the night, celebrated the eucharist the following morning, and after breakfast I
drove him to the airport. When in July 1990 news arrived of his
appointment to Canterbury, I wrote and was surprised, very
pleasantly of course, and greatly appreciative when I received an
altogether personal letter by way of acknowledgement.

It is now ten years since I retired from CCR[3] and returned to
Dublin, residing in the Milltown Park Jesuit community. During
this time I have been invited to occupy pulpits in a number of
Anglican churches in England and Ireland. I preached in the
Franciscan Friary at Hillfield on their Patronal Feast in
September 1994 , later that month in Coventry Cathedral and in
1996 in King's College Chapel, Cambridge. Here at home I have
preached at the Citizenship Service in Christ Church Cathedral
in November 1994, at Unity Week services in Castledermot
(1995), Clonakilty (1997), in the Cathedral Church of the Blessed
Trinity in Waterford (1999) and in Ballina in St Michael's (2002);
at a millennium service in St Patrick's Cathedral Dublin
(February 2000) and at a Memorial Service for Bishop McAdoo
in St Fin barre's Cathedral, Cork. (1999). On this occasion it was
moving to recall that at the end of the century I was preaching
from the same pulpit from which, at its beginning, John Gregg
delivered his famous series of six controversial sermons on 'The
Primitive Faith and Roman Catholic Developments'. That was
just ninety years previously (Lent 1909) – about the same time as
Mr Warren, our rector in Ardmore in the days of my youth, was
writing his controversial books and pamphlets.

In 1992 I had received an invitation from TCD to preach in
the College Chapel at a Quatercentenary Service of Thanksgiving. TCD was no longer forbidden territory for me as it had

---

3. I give an account of the origins of CCR in chapter 18 of *Christian
Unity: An Ecumenical Second Spring?* pp 317-340,394.

been in the 60s and I was happy to accept.[4] Things had indeed changed. And from the academic year 1982/3 duly qualified students of ISE became eligible for TCD's M. Phil degree. Things had changed on all sides. In my sermon I recalled how James II had wanted to hand TCD over to the Jesuits but was prevented by his Viceroy, the Earl of Tyrconnell who in a letter to the Queen had written that this would

> not only give great offence to all the world, I mean to England and Scotland, but very much discompose the whole clergy of this Kingdome, and madam, you know this age will not bear being too fond of Jesuits.

No age, it would seem, can, but TCD still gave me an honorary doctorate in 1995. And for a number of years I have been giving a short course of lectures at the Church of Ireland Theological College, not (as might perhaps have been expected) on 'Ecumenism and Catholicism', but on 'Ecumenism and Anglicanism' (sic). Bishop Donald Caird, when Rector of Rathmichael, did once introduce me to his parishioners as 'a Jesuit in whom there is no guile' – a backhanded compliment perhaps but a compliment none the less.

---

4. A somewhat abbreviated text is printed in the Winter 1992 issue of *Studies*, pp 399-407.

CHAPTER FOUR

Methodist Memories

'Friends of all and enemies of none': so the Methodists have always seen themselves. As far as Catholic-Methodist relations in general go, this ideal should have been somewhat easier to reach because in our case there never was a formal estrangement and parting of the ways; there are 'none of the historical, emotional problems consequent on a history of schism'. And in the early decades of the last century a leading British Methodist, Principal of the well-known evangelical institution, Cliff College in Derbyshire, did not hesitate to declare that if he had not been a Methodist, he would have been a Roman Catholic.[1]

It should have been easier still as far as Jesuit-Methodist relations go. Macaulay has a remark someplace to the effect that, had Ignatius of Loyola been in Oxford in the eighteenth century, he would have started the Methodists and that, had John Wesley been in Rome in the sixteenth, he would have started the Jesuits. This is a perceptive remark. Not only did the two men have a flair for method and organisation, there was a deep spiritual affinity between them.[2] One of the most striking examples is John Wesley's Covenant Service with its moving phrases: 'I am no longer my own, but yours ...' and the 'Take, Lord, and Receive ...' of the Spiritual Exercises of Ignatius of Loyola. I have read someplace that a former Principal of Cliff College used to recommend the lives of Jesuit saints to his Methodist students. I don't find this incredible but have not so far been able to confirm it.[3]

1. Norman G. Dunning, *Samuel Chadwick*, London,Hodder and Stoughton, 1934, p 19. Had he been a Catholic he would have liked to be 'the Abbot of a Monastery', ibid, p 20.
2. Cf Brendan Byrne,SJ, 'Ignatius Loyola and John Wesley: Experience and Strategies of Conversion', *Colloquium: The Australian and New Zealand Theological Review,19/1* (October 1986), pp 54-62.
3. It wasn't Samuel Chadwick who, as the previous footnote indicates,

In their early days but not any longer, not at least in the West, Jesuits did a lot of street preaching. The Methodists still do and it is thanks to a Methodist that I have had at least one experience of this ministry of street preaching. On a summer's evening in the 70s, at the invitation of Rev Dennis Cooke, then minister of Centenary and Leeson Park in Dublin, I took up position at the top of Grafton St under the Stephen's Green triumphal arch, the Boer War memorial to the Dublin Fusiliers. I can remember the evening well not only because I was nervous like a novice but also because at one point the well-known photographer, Bill Doyle, happened along. A young traveller girl covered with a shawl had appeared in front of the podium and, as I reached forward towards her with the microphone, encouraging her to contribute, Bill captured the moment. This is a 'Methodist memory' with a difference because I was doing under Methodist auspices what the first generation of Jesuits regularly did. It was Dennis, I might add at this stage, who many years later when he was Principal of Edgehill Theological College in Belfast began the process by which I was awarded an honorary doctorate by Queen's University in 1993.

Despite our initial advantages, Catholics and Methodists succumbed in due course to the prevailing Christian culture: we became opponents rather than partners or friends. And when eventually the ecumenical movement got under way in the last century, the traditional anti-Protestantism and anti-Romanism of our churches did not disappear overnight. In the 60s *Whither Methodism?*, the magazine of the so-called 'Irish Methodist Revival Movement', tended to berate the Methodist 'hierarchy' for welcoming me (with all my 'unrenounced Papist trappings of "beads and bunkum"') into Methodist fellowship. 'Not only did they fall for Hurley's smooth-talk – they gave him full support in his bid to weaken the true Methodist position.' 'Subtlety and intrigue have long been synonymous with the Jesuits and it is heart-breaking to watch them practise their art on a helpless

---

had Benedictine rather than Jesuit sympathies nor (as someone suggested to me) does it seem to have been Tom Meadley, not at least according to John Young's *Tom Meadley 'Speaking for Himself'* (Cliff College Publishing 1999).

Methodism'.[4] The reference is to the fact that my edition of John Wesley's *Letter to a Roman Catholic* which was published in 1968 appeared in these islands under the imprint not only of Geoffrey Chapman but also of Epworth House, Belfast, and in the USA under the imprint of Abingdon Press and with Prefaces by Bishop Odd Hagen, then President of the World Methodist Council, and by Cardinal Bea, President of what was then the Secretariat for Promoting Christian Unity in the Vatican.

Similar anti-ecumenical sentiments were expressed a few years later in a leaflet entitled *Church Member waken up. YOU ARE BEING BETRAYED.* This however was more overtly political: 'Do you know that unsuspecting church members and loyalists are being led towards a United Ireland by ecumenical Romanising Ministers?' Special reference was made to the fact that I had preached in St Patrick's Cathedral Dublin on St Patrick's Day 1972 and that 'Church of Ireland, Methodist and Presbyterian ministers were also at this service fellowshipping with this blasphemous, hypocritical Jesuit emissary of the Church of Rome.' The political situation was, of course, very tense in the aftermath of Bloody Sunday in Derry, the burning of the British Embassy in Dublin, the bombs at Aldershot and at the Abercorn restaurant in Belfast and just before the announcement of Direct Rule, of the suspension of Stormont. Church authorities were nervous and wary of ecumenical moves, and in the early 70s it was felt to be wiser that the students for the Methodist ministry did not meet me in Edgehill College itself but rather in the home of one of the students, the Rev Kenneth Thompson, who now very kindly looks back on this meeting as 'a seminal moment'.

If my edition of John Wesley's *Letter to a Roman Catholic* appeared with a Preface by Cardinal Bea, this did not happen without some difficulty, because I felt I had to return his first draft, a move which almost jeopardised the whole project and certainly delayed its completion.[5] If the edition appeared under the imprint of Epworth House Belfast this also did not happen without some difficulty, and were it not for the influence of Dr

---

4. *Whither Methodism?*, October-December 1968, p 3.
5. Cf below Chapter Six.

Eric Gallagher it would not have happened at all. When the Directors of the Irish Methodist Publishing Company met on 14 November 1967 to consider the joint publication, one of them wrote afterwards to say that 'we were unable to reach a unanimous decision and, pending further consideration of the matter, I am unable to give you an assurance that we will be able to proceed in the matter'. By the end of the month, however, they had reached a unanimous decision with the proviso that we 'use the imprint of "Epworth House, Belfast" rather than the Company imprint' and add a footnote to the effect that neither Geoffrey Chapman nor Epworth House, Belfast had 'any official connection with a church'. Eric Gallagher had been active in the meantime. He would continue until his death to be an active supporter of all ecumenical causes, as I have tried to express in a tribute to him published in the February 2000 issue of *Doctrine and Life*. 'Nothing happened,' I wrote there, 'of any significance for the cause of reconciliation in post-World War II and post-Vatican II Ireland without the active encouragement if not the actual participation of Eric Gallagher.'

The World Methodist Conference met in London in August 1966 and I was very fortunate to secure an appointment as an 'accredited visitor'. Just prior to the meeting, it had been announced that official talks were about to begin between the Vatican and the World Methodist Council. The initiative had been very largely the work of Bishop Fred Corson, then President of the Council and a very influential personality, but the news did not meet with any great enthusiasm in London. Indeed a specific reference in the Conference Message to relations with Catholics was in fact a late insertion and largely due to an intervention by Stanley Worrall, an Irish delegate who in his speech referred to a *Letter to a Roman Catholic* written by John Wesley from Dublin in 1749. I had never before heard of this document and came home determined to find it and study it. Unfortunately no copy of the original 1749 printing of the Letter seems to have survived any place in Ireland but I was greatly helped by Dr John Bowmer of the Methodist Archives and Research Centre in London who, among other things, provided me with a photocopy of the original 1749 printing.

It was my editing of John Wesleys' *Letter to a Roman Catholic* which led to my membership of The World Methodist Council/ Roman Catholic Church Joint Commission. Notwithstanding – or perhaps because of – the contretemps about his preface Cardinal Bea invited me to become a member. Methodists work in quinquennial periods and there were four annual meetings in each quinquennium. News of my appointment did not arrive in time for me to be present at the opening meeting near Rome in October 1967 but I did attend all three subsequent meetings and all four of the following quinquennium (1971-6) which ended with a meeting of the World Methodist Conference in Dublin in 1976.

Membership of the Commission brought us opportunities for travel at no financial loss and it would be less than honest not to acknowledge how welcome and agreeable these were. The seven meetings I attended took place in London (1968), in Rabat, Malta (1969), in Luka Junaluska, South Carolina, the GHQ or 'Vatican' of World Methodism (1970), in Rome (1972), in Reuti in the Bernese Oberland of Switzerland(1973), in Venice (1974) and in Bristol at Wesley College (1975). This last meeting was to have taken place in Lake Junaluska and we on this side of the Atlantic had been looking forward to another opportunity of visiting the USA. It was somewhat reluctantly, therefore, if quite readily that we agreed to meet in Bristol in order to accommodate Rev Raymond George who, being President that year of the British Methodist Conference, felt he couldn't afford to be out of the country, but whose presence, because of his theological compet- ence, we felt to be necessary.

Membership of the Commission broadened our horizons not only geographically but also spiritually. One thing became im- mediately obvious: neither side was a monolith. For Catholics, for myself at least, what we experienced for the first time was the difference between American Methodism and British-Irish Methodism. The 'district superintendents' we knew were 'bish- ops' in America and in due course it emerged that a Methodist bishop had the reputation of being even more authoritarian than a traditional Catholic bishop. When, therefore, some slight dis- agreements began to surface between me and our Catholic Co- Chairman, Archbishop Murphy of Cardiff during the first quin- quennium, it came as something of a surprise and a source subsequently of some discreet amusement among our Methodist friends in particular to find that, in the change of membership for the second quinquennium, it was the archbishop who was dropped and I who survived.

Broadening our spiritual horizons included of course having some of our misunderstandings corrected. For instance, membership of the Commission disabused us of the idea that theology was not a Methodist *forte*. The Americans did always seem to want to have as the first item on the agenda the day and time of departure and even the possibility of advancing these. But Bishop William Cannon was a fine mind and a fine theologian as well as a bit of a poet who every year composed his own verses for his annual Christmas card, and so of course was the ebullient Professor Albert Outler. The Methodist however whose theology impressed me most was Dr Harold Roberts of Cambridge. I shall never forget his address, positive and sympathetic with all the required theological and philosophical finesse, on the controversial topic of transubstantiation

I myself prepared two papers, one on 'The Church and Secularisation', the other on 'Salvation Today and Prevenient Grace'. We opened up for discussion many different subjects because the talks were exploratory. Our aim was not to draft a scheme of union, a marriage contract so to speak. Matrimonial language can be helpful in ecumenism as in other church matters. Our aim in those terms was rather to see whether the question of an engagement could be seriously considered and to that end to encourage our churches to begin or develop that interchurch courtship, that 'going steady' which consists in 'doing everything together as far as conscience permits', according to the principle formulated at an ecumenical conference in Lund in 1952.

Our 1968 London meeting had, therefore, suggested that we prepare reports on Catholic/Methodist relations in different areas. I prepared such a report with reference to Ireland, for our Malta meeting the following year. Skimming now through its twenty six pages, dated 11 September 1969, I find that under the stress of the current critical situation I was bold enough to suggest that the President of the English Methodist Conference, in his capacity as President of the Irish Conference, should take 'a

most serious interest in Irish affairs'; that like Westminster 'he'
(*sic*) and the English delegation should abandon the convention
of leaving Irish affairs to Ireland, should support the efforts of
Eric Gallagher and kindred spirits and so help the whole of Irish
Methodism 'to put its entire strength and influence into the
work of reconciliation'. It was the English Methodists, I even
suggested, who might have given the example to Westminster
and not *vice versa*.

My Report also brings back happy memories of the 60s and
in particular of the Glenstal and Greenhills Conferences. These
began in June 1964 and in January 1966 respectively and still
continue as annual unofficial ecumenical events. They are significant not only because they have survived the winter of ecumenism but also for two other reasons: their spiritual character
and their interdenominational/multilateral character. At Glenstal
we lived and prayed together. At Greenhills we prayed together.
Celebrations of the eucharist formed no part of the programme
in the first years but our non-eucharistic prayers made the conferences an exercise in spiritual ecumenism and this for many
was their most moving and rewarding feature.

The first Glenstal Conference had been conceived as an
Anglican/Catholic project, but the late Abbot Joseph Dowdall
and Fr Austin Flannery OP very graciously yielded to my suggestion and request that Methodists and Presbyterians also be
invited. Any exclusiveness seemed anathema in the first flush of
our ecumenical enthusiasm and the slender resources of all our
churches offered little prospect of separate bilateral meetings of
Catholics with Methodists and with Presbyterians. In the event,
what beforehand may have seemed to be too bold for a beginning, too likely to be an obstacle to real dialogue, proved rather
to be a help and an enrichment; and they paved the way for the
official multilateral conferences which nine years later began at
Ballymascanlon.

At the first Glenstal Conference, a paper on 'Pulpit and Table
in Methodism' was read by Rev Robert A. Nelson and at the first
Greenhills Conference the Rev A. D. Gilliland read a Methodist
'Comment' or response to a paper on the church by Kevin
McNamara, then a professor in Maynooth and not yet a bishop.
Both these men were former missionaries, the first in Sri Lanka,

the second in China. As such, they are somewhat typical of Protestant ecumenists, many of whom have a previous missionary experience and they raise again the interesting question why Catholic returned missionaries, unlike their Protestant counterparts, did not in general exhibit the same ecumenical zeal.

Desmond Gilliland and Robert Nelson took a particular interest in the Glenstal and Greenhills Conferences, specially in ensuring a good Methodist attendance. In those years Desmond was Minister of Centenary Church in Dublin and he had contributed to my Malta Report a moving, valuable piece about his family history and the pioneering work of his father, also a Methodist minister who had established good relations with his Catholic neighbours and who became a firm supporter of Muintir na Tíre, a post-World War II community organisation, and a good friend of its founder Canon John Hayes. Robert had just returned from Sri Lanka and in December 1963 on the publication of *Praying for Unity* had written me a very kind and warm letter to say: 'I am reading it with the greatest happiness and blessing and it will be very much with me during the days of Unity Week'. Among other things, Robert liked to recall from his own past how his father had refused to take part in the signing of the Solemn League and Covenant against Home Rule on Ulster Day, 28 September 1912.

My Malta Report, because of its date (11 September 1969), has nothing about the Irish School of Ecumenics (ISE) which came to dominate my horizons from the following year. Among those with whom I discussed the project and from whom I received encouragement were the Principal of Edgehill (the Methodist Theological) College, Rev Dr Richard Greenwood on 13 February, and the Secretary of the Irish Council of Churches who was the Methodist Minister, Rev Dr Norman Taggart, on 23 February. When the School was formally inaugurated on 9 November, the General Secretary of the World Council of Churches, Rev Dr Eugene Carson Blake was accompanied by the Northern Irish Methodist, then on the staff of WCC, Rev Wilbert Forker. From the very beginning, Robert Nelson and his wife Lorna were outstanding in their encouragement. Robert became Methodist Patron and was also a devoted member of both Council and Board.

The two outstanding achievements of ISE in my decade as Director were, apart from its survival, the International Consultations on Mixed Marriage in September 1973 and on Human Rights in December 1978. What might be called a third such achievement occurred during my Belfast years as ISE Lecturer in Continuing Education. This was the research project on 'Reconciliation in Religion and Society'. Methodist scholars were involved in all three. In the first, one of the main speakers was Rev Professor Geoffrey Wainwright, then in Queen's College, Birmingham; in the second, Professor Jose Miguez Bonino from Buenos Aires; and in the third Professor Wainwright again (though now in Duke University in the USA) and Professor Dennis Cooke, Principal of Edgehill College, Belfast.

Among other Methodists who generously helped ISE were Professor Wesley Cocker (TCD), Rev Kenneth Thompson and Mr Risteard Ó Glaisne who became members of Council or Board. Fred Jeffery of Methodist College, Belfast became a Trustee. Rev Ernest Gallagher (another returned missionary), when he became Minister of Centenary Church Dublin, helped as a fieldwork tutor. Rev Gordon Wakefield came from London to teach a course in our very first year, and Rev Dr Geoffrey Wainwright came more than once from Birmingham to do stints of teaching. Indeed I once hoped he would succeed me as Director.

One name conspicuous by its absence from this list is that of Rev Dr Eric Gallagher. In the early 80s he and Stanley Worrall wrote that

> The school [ISE], with patrons drawn from the mainstream bodies, had to struggle hard for survival in its early days against what at times could only be termed, at the most charitable, official apathy, and, from the traditionalists on each side of the divide, extreme hostility. (*Christians in Ulster*, 1968-1980, p 141)

But he himself was caught between a rock and a hard place. He would have wanted to support ISE as much as possible – he conveyed this to me more than once – and eventually on his retirement he did become actively involved: he worked hard to secure official recognition and in consequence some financial support from the main churches. In the early 70s, however, the politico-religious situation was extremely tense and in that situation efforts were being made to forge for the first time official contacts between the churches, in particular between the churches of the Irish Council of Churches and the Catholic Church. Eric Gallagher played a prominent part in these efforts and soon found out that Jesuits were not *personae gratae* to the Catholic Church authorities in the North and likewise ISE, especially after the Mixed Marriage Consultation. For the greater good, as he saw it, in order not to jeopardise the emerging official relationship with the Catholic Church and a consequent improvement in community relations, Eric wisely decided to postpone his support for ISE.

However when the Columbanus Community of Reconciliation was mooted in 1981 Eric and Norman Taggart and Ernest Gallagher (then Principal of Edgehill College) distinguished themselves in their support. One of Eric's particular contributions was to ask an architect friend to examine the building at 683 Antrim Road in Belfast which it was proposed to buy. The friend was an Orangeman. Unfortunately Ernest died prematurely in February 1984 but I was privileged to be invited by his widow, Muriel, and the family to give the address at his funeral service held in Dublin in Leeson Park Church. Norman was then Superintendent of the Belfast Central Mission where more than one meeting took place during the two years of the feasibility study 1981-3. The indebtedness of CCR to Methodism is perhaps most clearly illustrated by the fact that for the annual renewal of our promises we regularly used the Methodist Covenant Service. Eric and his wife Barbara, Norman and his wife Margaret were prodigal in the tender loving care which they showered on us. David Turtle and David Kerr were also strong supporters, unsparing in their helpfulness, the latter especially in CCR's last difficult years before it closed in 2002. Very appropriately it was Norman who gave the address on 15 September 2002 when the Columbanus Community held its closing service at 683 Antrim Road. It was he who had given the address when the Community held its inaugural service at the Belfast Central Mission on 15 September 1983. In the intervening years he had been in Sri Lanka and served as President of the Methodist Church in Ireland.

CHAPTER FIVE

Presbyterian Memories

Who to mention first? It is indeed *l'embarras du choix* but my first choice falls unhesitatingly on Donald Gillies, all the more so because *The Presbyterian Herald* was unable to find space for a tribute to him which I submitted around the time of his death. Donald's *Unity in the Dark* had appeared in 1964 arguing that the ecumenical movement 'bids to become the greatest menace to the truth of the Gospel since the time of the Reformation'. On 27 February 1996 I had written to the editor of *The Presbyterian Herald* as follows:

May I express to your readers and to the whole church my deep sympathy on the recent death of the Rev Donald Gillies?

I got to know Donald away back in late November 1965 when we were both members of a TV panel to discuss a book entitled *Rome: Opponent or Partner?* by Rudolf Ehrlich, then on the staff of New College, Edinburgh. We didn't, of course, quite agree during that programme. Donald, then as always, had the courage of his convictions and did not hesitate to tell our viewers that he was unable to recognise me as a Christian.

That was perhaps an unpromising beginning but it was a real beginning. Subsequently, after an exchange of Christmas cards, we met frequently but of course discreetly, mostly in Belfast but once or twice also here in Dublin. These meetings were the occasion for spirited theological conversations: nothing was more alien to Donald's systematic as well as evangelical mind than loose thinking.

Before too long Donald and I came to accept each other as friends. This friendship brought me much pleasure and profit; and I like to think that it also brought him some pleasure and profit. We became, I feel sure, more than friends: we grew in appreciation not only of each other but of each other's Christian tradition; we became 'friends in the Lord'. And Donald, believing in deed as well as word that light can come 'from any quarter', had the courage to modify his views on ecumenism and on Rome and in the 70s to support the Presbyterian Church's continuing membership of the World Council of Churches. His life encourages all of us to be open to the Spirit and ready for change so that the world may believe and be at peace.

Donald was a theologian, though too 'scholastic' for me, and I've often thought and said that, were I to envisage changing my church allegiance, I'd become a Presbyterian. For Calvin, the teacher, the 'doctor' was one of the four orders in the ministry of the church. This may no longer be part of the Presbyterian doctrine of the church but theology is still held in high honour among Presbyterians, in particular systematic as distinct from historical theology. Being myself a theologian manqué, having 'laid waste my powers' in administration and fundraising I appreciate all the more the value and importance of systematic theology

In my education as a Presbyterian two major experiences stand out in my memory. The first was my participation in the Summer of 1964 in the nineteenth General Council of the World Presbyterian Alliance at Frankfurt, discussing the theme of Renewal. This plunged me into the international scene, showing me that the ecumenical problems of Irish Presbyterians were not so peculiarly Irish. I was greatly impressed by the emphasis on the Holy Spirit and the generous attitude taken to Presbyterian/ Catholic relations. What I remember best is the opening sermon by the Rev Dr W. A. Visser 't Hooft, General Secretary of the World Council of Churches. 'It would seem,' he said (basing himself on Acts 4:31) 'that in our time the Spirit is again shaking the place in which the church finds itself' and he went on to ask: 'Have we realised that renewal can only be renewal by the Holy Spirit and that such renewal means precisely to be shaken up?'

The second major experience in my Presbyterian education was the opportunity of reading and studying the Fourth Book of Calvin's *Institutes*. An invitation had come from the Maynooth

Summer School to do a paper on 'The Church in Protestant Theology' for their 1965 session. Articles that had appeared in 1964 on the occasion of the fourth centenary of Calvin's death, one especially by the Methodist scholar, Gordon Rupp, had suggested that the Fourth Book of the *Institutes* was a rich but neglected source, neglected even by the Presbyterians themselves. Following up this lead, the paper I prepared for Maynooth carried the subtitle 'Some Reflections of the Fourth Book of Calvin's *Institutes*'.

The Fourth Book deals with 'The External Means or Aids by which God invites us into the Society of Christ and holds us Therein'. It made a profound impression on me and on my eventual audience. It was quite a revelation. As at Frankfurt, I was once again impressed by the emphasis on the Holy Spirit. I found that the book contained of course an anti-Roman trend, as expected, but also an anti-Anabaptist, anti-Zwinglianist and anti-Lutheran trend, and indeed that these three latter had profoundly influenced Calvin's thinking. So much so that – to my surprise – he lays very considerable stress on visible structures and visible unity, on sacraments and liturgy, on the real eucharistic presence. The church's ministry of word, sacrament and discipline, as he saw it, is not an intermediary coming between us and our Saviour. It is a mediation of Christ's own word and life and authority. The church and her ministers receive from the ascended Christ the gift of the Holy Spirit and in him become an effectual 'exhibition' of Christ: his visible efficacious presence on earth till the Lord comes. Of course as Brian McConnell, then Minister of Donore here in Dublin, and other Presbyterian friends would remind me, the writings of the Reformers are not even subordinate standards of belief; Calvin is not as important for Presbyterians as Wesley is for Methodists.

The middle years of the 60s have been referred to by former Moderator, Dr John Dunlop, as 'the short period of hope'. These were the years when Vatican II was meeting (1962-5) and delegate-observers were present from almost all the other churches helping us to renew and reform ourselves, and the Presbyterian editor of *Biblical Theology* commissioned an article from me about it which appeared in the October issue of 1963. These were the years when Carlisle Patterson was influential in the

The author being ordained by Bishop (later Cardinal) Suenens
on 15 August 1954 at Eegenhoven-Louvain.

Ardmore, Co Waterford, the author's home
(Photo: Kevin F. Dwyer, Glanmire, Cork. Used by kind permission.)

The author street preaching at Stephen's Green Dublin
in the 1960s

On 18 November 1964 at a Milltown Park Lecture, the author who was
lecturer that evening, with his Excellency President de Valera and the
Jesuit Provincial, Fr Charles O'Conor

In June 1968 Rev Ian Paisley outside Church House in Belfast
on the occasion of the Presbyterian General Assembly,
protesting against the authorities of Assembly's College
for having invited the author to lecture the students

9 November 1970, the formal inauguration of the Irish School of Ecumenics at Milltown Park Dublin. Left to right: Rev Mícheál Mac Gréil SJ, Rev Maurice Stewart, Rev Gabriel Daly OSA, Rev Dr James Boyd, Rev Professor John Barkley, the author, Rev Dr Carson Blake, General Secretary, World Council of Churches who gave the inaugural address, the Right Rev Richard Hanson, Church of Ireland Bishop of Clogher, Rev David Clarke, Rev Ernest Gallagher and Rev Robert N. Brown

15 April 1970 in the chapel of Gonzaga College, Dublin on the occasion of the presentation of *Irish Anglicanism 1869-1969* to the Church of Ireland. From left: Rev Robert Nelson, Chairman of Dublin Methodist District and Secretary of the Dublin Council of Churches, Rev Cecil McGarry, Jesuit Provincial and Vice-Chancellor of Milltown Institute, Rev Professor J. L. M. Haire, Principal, Assembly's College, Belfast, Rev Declan Deane SJ, Archbishop George Simms and the author.

In July 1971 at a press conference to announce the link between the
University of Hull and the Irish School of Ecumenics.
From left: Sir Brynmor Jones, Vice-Chancellor, the author,
Right Rev John W. Armstrong, Church of Ireland Patron of ISE,
and Rev Professor Anthony Hanson, Department of Theology,
University of Hull.

On the occasion of the publication in 1980 of the proceedings of the ISE
Human Rights Consultation, from left: Rev Alan D. Falconer, editor,
Seán MacBride, one of the contributors, and the author.

November 1983 at the inauguration of the Columbanus Community of Reconciliation at 683 Antrim Road, Belfast, from left: the author, Rev Dr Eric Gallagher, formerly President, Methodist Church in Ireland, and Cardinal Tomás Ó Fiaich.

In May 1993, at the launch of *Reconciliation: Essays in Honour of Michael Hurley* at Trinity College Dublin, from left: Rev Derek Ritchie, President, Methodist Church in Ireland, Rev Oliver Rafferty SJ, editor, the author, Right Rev John Dunlop, Moderator of General Assembly, Presbyterian Church in Ireland and the two archbishops of Armagh, Cardinal Cahal Daly and Archbishop Robin Eames.

July 1995, the author with theologian Professor Hans Küng
and poet Derek Mahon
on the occasion of their honorary doctorates
from Trinity College Dublin

In October 1998, the author with Cardinal Cassidy,
President of the Pontifical Council for Promoting Christian Unity,
who was in Dublin and Belfast to launch the author's collection,
Christian Unity: An Ecumenical Second Spring?

Presbyterian Inter-Church Relations Committee/Board and promoting a more generous ecumenical policy. With his encouragement a Faith and Order Conference at Greystones in 1963 called on all the Irish Protestant churches 'to consider in what ways we ought to respond in truth and love to our Roman Catholic brethren who express their sense of fellowship with us'. And during General Assembly that year, William Montgomery as Moderator invited the members to stand in silence as a mark of respect to Pope John XXIII who had just died. (The Union Jack was also flown at half mast on City Hall in Belfast.) He also very kindly contributed a generous 'Introductory Message' to my *Praying for Unity* which appeared later that year.

Carlisle also greatly influenced a resolution passed by the 1965 Presbyterian General Assembly urging its members 'humbly and frankly to acknowledge and to ask forgiveness for any attitudes and actions towards our Roman Catholic fellow-countrymen which have been unworthy of our calling as followers of Jesus Christ'. I devoted one of my bi-monthly articles in *The Furrow* (August 1965) to an appreciation of this resolution, noting that 'to my knowledge no other church at home or abroad has as yet considered or passed such a resolution as this'. In his memoirs published in 1997, Carlisle sees the resolution as 'the most remarkable sign that the old order of things could not survive even within Irish Presbyterianism ... even thirty years later [it] reads as a very remarkable pronouncement'. Carlisle's decision to transfer to England and work from 1970 with the Conference of British Missionary Societies was a serious loss to the ecumenical movement in Ireland.

The mid-sixties were also the years in which the Glenstal (June 1964) and Greenhills (January 1966) conferences began. Although originally conceived as an Anglican/Catholic gathering, the late Abbot of Glenstal, Dom Joseph Dowdall, and Fr Austin Flannery OP readily agreed (as mentioned in the last chapter) to my request that Methodists and Presbyterians also be included. It was a risk but it succeeded and was never regretted. The Presbyterians who in the early years helped to muster some of their colleagues were Alec Smyth and Brian McConnell. Alec, The Very Rev T. A. B. Smyth, a former Moderator and an expert on roses, was in the 60s and 70s Minister of Rathgar

Presbyterian Church, Dublin. Brian, the Rev G. B. G. McConnell, was then Minister of Donore, a frequent correspondent to the daily papers on national and international affairs; he had a flair for controversy and has recently published his memoirs under the title *Memoirs of an Unrepentant Liberal*. Alec and Brian were great encouragers of us Catholics as we took our first uncertain steps in the ways of ecumenism. As members of the Glenstal and Greenhills organising committees, they were responsible for ensuring a Presbyterian presence and choosing the particular person when a Presbyterian seemed appropriate. The Presbyterian speaker at Glenstal in 1964 was Desmond Bailie. Alec himself read a paper on 'The Holy Communion in the Reformed Tradition' at the second Glenstal conference in 1965. At Glenstal in 1966 Professor John M. Barkley and Professor J. L. M. Haire both read papers; in the following decades both played prominent parts in supporting the Irish School of Ecumenics and the Columbanus Community of Reconciliation. .

Unfortunately, the Greenhills conference led one year to a sharp exchange of letters between me and some Presbyterian authorities. I had conceived the idea of the four church leaders (the two Archbishops of Armagh, the Methodist President and the Presbyterian Moderator) coming, not to attend the sessions but, in between the sessions, to join us for lunch on the day of the Greenhills conference and by this gesture encouraging ecumenical togetherness. My files contain a letter from Cardinal Conway dated 15 August 1966; he for his part is agreeable to the idea and to an approach being made to the other three. The next letter in my files is dated 4 July 1968 and is from the current Presbyterian Moderator, the Right Rev John H. Withers. A few years previously Dr Withers had invited a Catholic priest to address a group of his congregation, to the great fury of Dr Paisley. Knowing his ecumenical spirit I had apparently invited him to the lunch at Greenhills in Unity Week 1969; he had accepted but later withdrawn his acceptance (The relevant correspondence is not in my files). His letter of July 1968 is in response to one of mine which seemed to him like 'a vehement rebuke' for his 'second thoughts'. This letter of 4 July 1968 confirms and explains his decision not to attend. He had 'impetuously accepted' my 'gracious invitation, without the courtesy of first consulting those who, over the years, have, with you, been equally committed to the Conference'. His presence would convey an impression of 'officiality'. My files contain two other letters which are relevant. One dated 20 January 1969 is from the Clerk of Assembly, Rev A. J. Weir developing very calmly Dr Withers' reasons for declining to attend the luncheon and a copy of my response to this letter dated 6 February 1969. This is somewhat aggressive in tone and feebly attempts to justify this with a reference to 'ecumenical parrhesia'.

Dr John Dunlop saw his 'short period of hope' ending in 1968. It was in October of that year that the Troubles really began with the Civil Rights march in Derry. That summer a motion censuring the authorities of Assembly's College for having me lecture the students on Baptism the previous February was debated – and defeated – in General Assembly, while outside Dr Paisley and his followers had protested, carrying placards 'Jesuit Hurley teaches in Assembly's College'. That is the context, the highly charged atmosphere, in which the above correspondence has to be read. 1968 and 1969 did eventually see the four church leaders having their first meeting, but it would have been provocative to hold this at one of the ecumenical gatherings which were such a bone of contention because they were seen by many as indicating 'a Romeward trend' in Presbyterianism and Protestantism in general. I had been out of the country for the first half of 1967 when Dr Paisley had succeeded in blocking a lecture on Vatican II by Church of England Bishop Moorman. I wasn't sufficiently sensitive to the impending crisis. Anything like a 'vehement rebuke' was certainly altogether out of place.

In the latter years of the 60s, I was busy with the arrangements for the launch of *Irish Anglicanism* which took place in April 1970, and for the launch of the Irish School of Ecumenics which took place in November of the same year. Sadly, the latter brought me into conflict with that year's Moderator, the Right Rev J. L. M. (Jimmie) Haire, Principal of Assembly's College. He it was who had invited me to lecture his students on Baptism as I had invited him to lecture mine on Original Sin (in Autumn 1966). He it was who had taken a prominent part in the interdenominational service held on the occasion of the launch of *Irish Anglicanism* and who had invited me as one of his guests on the occasion of his installation as Moderator in June. I had to accept, however reluctantly, his decision to absent himself from the inauguration ceremonies. It is an accepted fact that the constraints of office often oblige authorities, both civil and religious, to follow the prevailing rather than their personal view. But there was also a suggestion that the invitation to Rev Dr Eugene Carson Blake, a Presbyterian and General Secretary of the World Council of Churches to give the inaugural lecture be withdrawn. Opposition to their membership of the WCC was growing among Presbyterians because of its Programme to Combat Racism which was viewed as support for terrorism and implicitly for the IRA.. The withdrawal of the invitation to Dr Carson Blake I resisted on the grounds, among others, that it would be another Ripon case, strengthening still further the hand of Dr Paisley. It was all a very unpropitious start to ISE. I have on file a letter from Jimmie dated 25 July 1970 and a copy of my response of 17 August. This I signed 'Yours brokenheartedly' and happily our friendly relationship survived the incident.

As a result of the constraints on Jimmie Haire, it was Professor John M. Barkley who became Presbyterian Patron of ISE. John was a faithful supporter of the Glenstal and Greenhills Conferences; he contributed to *Irish Anglicanism*, he generously came from Belfast to do stints of teaching in ISE and to attend Council meetings, and in 1977 he declined the honour and office of Moderator of General Assembly because, among other reasons, it would inhibit his religious freedom as an ecumenist. It was therefore with the greatest of pleasure and 'with affection' that I dedicated to his memory my essay on 'The Preparatory Years' in the volume *The Irish Inter-Church Meeting*, commemorating in 1998 the twenty-fifth anniversary of this ecumenical agency which includes the Catholic Church as a member.

Two particular memories of John come to mind. He reminded us Catholics – and we needed reminding – that we weren't the only Christians to be persecuted in Ireland, that Presbyterians had also suffered from the penal laws, that they resented in particular the Anglican denial in the past of the validity of their marriages and the legitimacy of their children. The second memory is the way he made clear to us at Glenstal in 1966 the exact meaning which 'sprinkling' has for Protestants in the administration of baptism. 'The minister dips his hand in the water and allows the water to fall on the head of the candidate.' This explanation and actual demonstration, showing how for them the meaning of 'sprinkling' was different from what it was for us, put to rest our hesitations and doubts about the validity of baptism by 'sprinkling' in the other churches, as if 'sprinkling' was a rather 'hit-and-miss' affair.

Other Presbyterians who contributed significantly to the development of ISE were Miss Margaret Hamilton Reid who became and remains a Trustee, the Rev Alistair Heron of the Church of Scotland who was our first staff appointment and whose research and writing on mixed marriages contributed greatly to the success of the International Consultation in 1974; Rev Alan Falconer, also of the Church of Scotland who succeeded Alistair, who was largely responsible for the 1978 International Consultation on Human Rights and who became Director of ISE before moving to Geneva to Faith and Order; Robin Boyd who succeeded me as Director in 1980 and whose Northern Ireland background and Indian experience as missionary and theologian and gracious, gentle presence brought ISE safely through its difficult adolescent years. The Presbyterian scholars who later in 1993 generously collaborated in the 'Reconciliation in Religion and Society' project were Duncan B. Forrester of New College, Edinburgh and J. Cecil McCullough, Professor of New Testament at Union Theological College (previously Assembly's College), Belfast and later its Principal.

ISE's indebtedness to Presbyterians includes above all perhaps the presentation made to it by Alec Smyth: a crucifix with a special history which continues to be on display in the entrance to the ISE's premises and which I referred to at the formal inauguration as our 'most cherished possession'. Quite surprisingly this crucifix belonged to the Very Reverend Andrew Gibson, MC, DD, a former Moderator of General Assembly and was presented to ISE by Dr Gibson's son at Alec Smyth's suggestion. As a chaplain in World War I Dr Gibson had found the crucifix in the mud and rubble of an unidentified French village and, having failed to find the owner, brought it back to Ireland and gave it a place of honour in the study of his Cork manse for twenty-one years.

Like ISE, the Columbanus Community of Reconciliation owed much to the encouragment of many Presbyterians. Jimmie Haire became its first Presbyterian Patron; he presided at our first Covenant Service in January 1984; later that year, in October, he conducted the first Visitation of the Community on behalf of his fellow Trustees; he enabled us to obtain practical advice and shelving for the Library from the Queen's University, Belfast Library and he himself donated a number of his own books; and it was he who formally received the Rt Hon The Lord Mayor of Belfast, Councillor Alfred H. Ferguson, when he came on 12 May 1985 to mark the completion of renovations to our house at 683 Antrim Road. Sadly, Jimmie died on 1 July 1985; I was greatly honoured to be invited by his widow ,Margaret and the family, to read a scripture passage at the interment.

Tom Patterson, Margaret Wilkinson, David Lapsley and John Dunlop contributed enormously to the beginnings and development of CCR. Tom, a former Moderator, a deeply spiritual man, passionately concerned about sectarianism, became a member of the interchurch committee which in the second year of the feasibility study produced a brochure outlining the shape and ethos of CCR, took part in interviewing candidates for membership, presided at the inauguration service celebrated on Columbanus Day, 23 November 1983, and for many years served as Chairman of the Trustees. He was succeeded in this position by fellow-Presbyterian, Mr James Russell, LLB.

Margaret was a founder member. Retired after many years as a missionary in South India with the Dohnavur Fellowship, membership of CCR was suggested to her by Tom. Being a conservative evangelical Margaret was a specially welcome member; she kept us balanced in our ways, committed to a pattern of prayer half-fixed and half-free, acting as a bridge with her fellow evangelicals so that Bertie Dickinson in his year as Moderator (1985-6) came to visit us.

David Lapsley was Minister of Fisherwick, successor to Jack Withers whom I had offended in the 60s. John Dunlop was and still is Minister of the Rosemary Congregation, CCR's local Presbyterian Church. Before Christmas of our first year, John invited us to a special meeting of his Elders to introduce ourselves and answer questions; subsequently we received a gracious letter of welcome from the Clerk of Session. David and John remained strong supporters. Both gave us every encouragement.

CCR has now folded after some twenty years. The weekend before our formal inauguration on 23 November 1983, the Darkley massacre happened. Republican terrorists had broken into a Pentecostal church at Darkley in Co Armagh while a service was on, killing three and wounding seven others. Two years later, on Columbanus Day itself, a huge crowd converged on the City Hall in Belfast to protest against the Anglo-Irish Agreement. The Troubles continued and in a real sense continue even after the Belfast Agreement. CCR did not bring the Troubles to an end. That was not its aim. Its aim was rather to challenge the sectarianism, injustice and violence prevalent in Northern Ireland and elsewhere in our world, to do so in deed not just in word, to give a practical example of integrated living, of what a more united church, a more just society and a more peaceful world could be like, to give encouragement to those commited to an improvement in interchurch relations. With that more modest aim, many feel that it may indeed have done much good during its short life.

CHAPTER SIX

Catholic Memories
Part I: Pre-1970

My first Catholic memories are ecumenical, in this sense at least, that my native village of Ardmore in Co Waterford had, as already mentioned in chapter three, its Church of Ireland church and rector, and therefore the existence of Christians other than Catholics was brought naturally to my attention. These Christians were different, of course, and somewhat distant – tending to be gentry from the Blackwater Valley – and we didn't attend their church, and in the past they had something to do with the penal laws. However, they were no longer seen as unwelcome intruders but as neighbours and the religion I imbibed at home and in the community was in no way sectarian or anti-Protestant or controversial.

As mentioned briefly in chapter two, two Catholic priests figure largely in the happy memories of my youth. The first was a diocesan, Fr Henry Synnott, who was our curate. I remember him as an outgoing, imaginative priest: he had a scheme by which the local farmers would help 'the foreign missions' not by contributing money directly but by sowing crops for them and then making the proceeds from the yield their contribution to the Propagation of the Faith. Though somewhat gruff and forbidding in appearance, he was a frequent visitor to our home; he often took us out fishing with him in his boat and packed us into his two-seater to go swimming at Goat Island, a nearby beach; he also played cards with us, rummy mostly; and more than once the game had to be interrupted to give him the opportunity of finishing his breviary before midnight. He presented me with a copy of the commentary on the fourth gospel, *The Gospel according to St John* by the Anglican scholar, Bishop B. F. Wescott (a remarkable ecumenical gesture surely in those pre-Vatican II days) and he joined the family at my ordination in Louvain and our subsequent tour around Europe. If I did as a boy think of becoming a priest, it was surely owing in some measure to his influence, but he never brought the subject up in conversation.

The second priest was a religious, the Cistercian, Fr Finbarr Cashman who was Junior Dean during my years in Melleray (1935-40). The Senior Dean looked and was stern. For the school Finbarr was the gentle face of authority, of discipline. We became fond friends and during holidays corresponded regularly, usually in Irish. If I did once think seriously of becoming a Cistercian it may well have been because of his influence but he never once spoke to me about joining the monastery. Fr Finbarr later became Abbot of Mount Melleray.

My Catholic memories from 1940 to the late 50s are largely Jesuit memories, no less happy for that but no more ecumenical either. These were the years of my 'formation' which aimed to make me a Jesuit. They were traumatic years for the whole world, for Europe in particular. I entered the novitiate just as the London blitz was beginning – but strangely, if not scandalously, we were kept out of touch for the most part with the earth-shattering changes taking place. Segregation from the 'world' was the order of the day. In any case, I allowed myself to become engrossed in the 'trivial pursuits' of noviceship life, accepting that 'indoor works' and 'outdoor works' interspersed of course with periods of prayer, were the stuff of sanctity. I then dutifully gave myself to the study of the classics in the safe environs of University College, Dublin at Earlsfort Terrace but, though quite successful in the mechanics of translating Greek and Latin, I never quite managed to get caught up in the glory which was Greece or the grandeur that was Rome. The following three years of philosophy in Tullabeg near Tullamore, in the remote reaches of a midland bog (the Jesuits had established a school there in the 19th century to be out of sight of government eyes) also failed to enthuse me. But I did learn to write and had a few articles published in *The Irish Monthly* and one accepted for publication by the *Gregorianum* in Rome.

1948 brought a change: teaching for three years in Mungret College, the Jesuit boarding school in Limerick and then studying theology in Louvain. My main memory of the Mungret years is of an anti-communist and anti-socialist atmosphere. There was, for instance, revulsion at the treatment of Cardinal

Mindzenty and opposition to the government's Mother and Child Scheme. I suffered as a result. One sign that I was by now recovering my zest for life (coincidentally Mungret had as its motto 'renewing my youth like that of an eagle') was the fact that I proposed a study circle on *The Communist Manifesto* to the senior boys and, though we would have to meet during the time for recreation and for smoking, a number readily agreed.

All went happily, apparently. But to get materials for the study circle I had no choice but to visit the Communist Bookshop in Pearse St, Dublin. Greatly daring I did so, wearing of course my clericals including hat, and feeling as I might now if I were to visit a sex shop. I was right to feel apprehensive because (sign of the anti-communist atmosphere of the times) the shop was under police surveillance. This transpired when a few days later a Garda came to Mungret enquiring about me. How I was recognised and traced in those pre-computer days I don't understand (was I followed to Limerick on the train?) but traced I was. Fortunately Fr Charles Heron, then Minister or Vice-Rector, was able to reassure the guards of my patriotism and of my orthodoxy and fortunately no action was taken against me by my Jesuit superiors for this indiscretion or misdemeanour.[1]

In retrospect I can now see that the one quite new element in my life during the four years of theology was its ecumenical dimension. Muintir na Tíre, the well-known community organisation founded by Canon John Hayes on a very broad basis, had held a Summer School at Mungret in my time and this had attracted a number of Protestants including the Church of Ireland Bishop of Limerick. But for the most part, in Ireland in these years we were indifferent to ecumenism; the churches had no felt need of each other. We all felt self-sufficient.

On the continent the war, among other things, had changed all that. In Louvain, I discovered the January Unity Week which we observed, though not on an interdenominational basis. I discovered, through the interest of one of our lecturers, the existence of the religious life in Anglicanism and Lutheranism and of

---

1. It is only in the last few years that I have heard of this incident. I heard of it from Fr James FitzGerald, then on the staff of Mungret (now in Gardiner St, Dublin) and a close friend of Fr Charlie Heron who died prematurely in the late 50s in Belvedere College.

course in Orthodoxy; he had visited Mount Athos. I discovered that Fr Synnott's gift of Westcott's *The Gospel According to St John* was a prophetic gesture; much of our recommended reading consisted of what might previously have been called 'forbidden books'. The stirrings of the aggiornamento which Pope John XXIII would canonise in the next decade were already to be felt. I pursued my social interests by contacts with the Young Christian Workers and a visit to the coalmines at Charleroi, and also by contacts with the Worker Priests in France and a few weeks working in a steel factory. However the shadow of *Humani Generis*, the encyclical of 1950 discouraging and indeed condemning certain trends in theology, was still over us. But the French style of putting statements in the form of questions *(on peut se demander si ...)* and thereby giving them a tentative character was no longer just the humility of the scholar appealing to his peers but the discretion of the priest looking over his shoulder.

After postgraduate work in Rome (1956-8), where I heard the great Bishop Bell (who failed to be appointed to Canterbury because of his criticism of the bombing of Dresden) give a lecture shortly before his death, I was appointed to teach systematic theology at Milltown Park, Dublin. The student body was confined to Jesuits and Carmelites preparing for the priesthood. So my first initiative was to suggest the series of public lectures on topical subjects of theological interest which proved to be the – altogether unplanned – beginning of my ecumenical apostolate.

The Milltown Park Public Lectures were a great success and continued twice a year, with two seven night sessions, from 1960 until 1981. There was a genuine interest in religion, whetted no doubt by Vatican II and the accounts of its proceedings appearing in the media; and as yet the competition from television was negligible. The large attendances included many members of other churches, notably perhaps Mrs Mercy Simms, wife of the archbishop, always ready to defend Archbishop McQuaid when he was criticised. The media response to the lectures was very positive and generous and Veritas published the text of my *Christian Unity* lecture as a pamphlet. What I remember most about that is a letter from Bishop Mageean of Down and Connor written in his own hand and in the green ink he customarily (so I gather) used – a letter of appreciation and thanks which unfortunately seems lost. In his 1961 Lenten Pastoral to his priests and people he wrote: 'I cordially commend it to you to read and study'. In 1959 Bishop Mageean had agreed to Catholic membership of the Churches' Industrial Council in Belfast.

Looking back now on the 60s, I would have no hesitation in saying that Canon J. G. McGarry, editor of *The Furrow*, was the person who gave me most encouragement. I seem to remember long telephone conversations with him on Saturday afternoons over a number of years. His January 1963 issue, devoted to the subject of Christian Unity, included three contributions from leading members of the other churches. He involved me in choosing them and invited me to do a reflection on their contributions. He also invited me to edit a book on the Unity Octave, entitled *Praying for Unity*. This was published in December 1963 by The Furrow Trust and Gill & Son, with a Foreword by Bishop Philbin of Down and Connor and Introductory Messages from the Church of Ireland Archbishop of Dublin, the Methodist President and the Presbyterian Moderator. For the two years 1965 and 1966, I contributed a bi-monthly short piece under the general title of 'Ecumenical Chronicle' which was meant to deal with the practice of ecumenism. The Greenhills Ecumenical Conference was Canon McGarry's idea: a January Unity Week meeting at a venue convenient to both North and South, and he himself identified an ideal location: the Presentation School near Drogheda in the diocese of Armagh. I remained involved in this for many years. It still survives.

Other Catholic confrères who gave me encouragement in my ecumenical apostolate[2] in the 60s were the late Abbot Joseph Dowdall of Glenstal, Mgr Tom Fehily and the late Mgr Cathal McCarthy. As previously mentioned in chapter four, the Abbot in 1964 generously agreed to my suggestion that the Church of Ireland/Catholic Conference being considered and arranged by himself and Fr Austin Flannery OP be opened up to include Methodists and Presbyterians. This was a risky step but it succeeded and the Conference still continues as an annual summer

---

2. And also Archbishop Scanlon of Glasgow. I have in my papers an *Ad Clerum* of his summoning the clergy to come for a two day seminar on ecumenism to be addressed by Fr Des Wilson of Belfast and myself early in 1968.

event. During the 60s Mgr Fehily, in his capacity as Director of the Dublin Diocesan Adult Education Centre, organised courses of evening lectures throughout the archdiocese and arranged transport for the lecturers. 'The Ecumenical Council and the Ecumenical Movement' was my favourite topic for a number of years. In 1964, for instance, I spoke on it in Aughrim, Co Wicklow on 5 October and in Castledermot, Co Carlow on 26 October. In 1965 Mgr McCarthy, then PP of Beechwood and liaison officer between Archbishop McQuaid and Radio Telefis Eireann, invited me to give a series of radio talks of some 25 minutes each on 'The Ecumenical Spirit' on the Sundays of Lent. According to the protocol of the time, I was expected to submit my texts to him in advance: I always found him most courteous. The protocol, however, led to some peculiar situations. Seán MacRéamoinn gave me my first introduction to television during Unity Week 1962 with a straight talk to camera. I didn't have to submit a text either to Seán or the archdiocese. But later, during discussions of the proceedings of Vatican II in which I frequently took part, an appointee of the archdiocese sat behind the scenes as a censor. This might have made some sense when the sessions were pre-recorded but not when they were going out live. I once got a letter of reprimand from Bishop Philbin of Down and Connor for giving an interview on BBC/NI without due permission from him.

The 60s were exciting times and also happy times for the most part. Unfortunately some unhappy incidents also occurred and two of them are 'Catholic Memories' associated in my mind with the Milltown Park Public Lectures. In October 1962 Fr Martin Brennan SJ lectured on 'Adam and Anthropology'. The First Session of Vatican II had just got under way and was not going according to the plans of the more conservative bishops. The press reports of this lecture duly reached Archbishop McQuaid as well, probably, as reports of these reports, and can have only added to his disquiet. The atmosphere in Rome was tense and the archbishop imposed a form of ecclesiastical censorship on us. On his return in early December he would 'reas-

3. Cf my *Christian Unity: An Ecumenical Second Spring?* pp 245-7, 387 (note 29).

4. As described above in the chapter on 'Methodist Memories'.

sure' the archdiocese stating that 'No change will disturb the
tranquillity of your Christian lives'. The imposed censorship
was an anticipation of this policy. It could, however, have been
worse. The lectures might have been stopped. Prior approval
might have been required for the names of proposed lecturers.
The censorship imposed applied not to the speakers or their top-
ics but to our press releases, which had to be submitted for prior
approval to Mgr Eugene Boylan of Dúnlaoire. This was a very
considerable practical inconvenience because the days of wordprocessing, fax and e-mail were far in the future; we didn't even
have a community car. But in general Mgr Boylan was helpful.

In one case, however, the censorship led to the last minute
cancellation of the lecture. I myself was the announced speaker
and my topic was 'Original Sin'. This was not until 1968 and
meantime I had already incurred the displeasure of the archbishop. An article of mine on 'Mixed Marriages' had appeared
in the May 1966 issue of *The Furrow,* and the editor of *The Irish
Times,* having received the required permission, announced in
his issue of Saturday 12 May that the paper would be reprinting
the article the following week. That weekend turned out to be an
agonising time. The archbishop phoned the provincial (he never
dealt directly with ordinary members of the order) who phoned
me asking me to withdraw my permission for the reprint. This
meant contacting the editor of *The Furrow* who owned the copy-
right. Fr McGarry was all sympathy and concern and, despite
his reservations, unwilling to make matters more awkward for
the provincial or for me. I then had to contact Mr Douglas Gageby
and make my request. There was no need for explanations, he
knew immediately what must have happened and who was behind the request. He promised to think about it when out walking on the Sunday afternoon. Though the article was probably
already in print he really had no choice, but he did leave me in
agony. Early in the week I had to go to Switzerland for a conference . The article never appeared but while I was away the second leader in the paper on Thursday, 19 May was entitled 'Silent
Dialogue?'

> Father Hurley is a man under discipine. One would not want
> to press him as to the reasons for his urgent request, or,
> rather for the name of the authority who instructed him to

make the request; but one is free to deplore the fact that it was made … How wrong, how old-fashioned and how damaging is that view [that ideas can still be hedged in].

Two years later the archbishop intervened to cause a lecture of mine on 'Original Sin' to be cancelled. But it was the lesser of two evils. I had lectured the theology students on the subject in St Paul University, Ottawa as well as in Milltown Park and an article of mine had passed the censors and appeared in *The Clergy Review*. But my press release obviously hadn't been circumspect enough. As a result the archbishop expressed the wish that the lecture be cancelled and that I no longer function in his diocese. The provincial was ready to acquiesce in this until my rector, Cecil McGarry intervened. He went personally to see the archbishop and a compromise was reached. I would continue to function in the diocese but my public lecture on Original Sin would be cancelled.[3] Without this intervention of Cecil McGarry how different my subsequent life would have been!

1968 was also the year in which my edition of John Wesley's *Letter to a Roman Catholic* was jointly published by a Catholic and a Methodist house and with prefaces by Bishop Odd Hagen, President of the World Methodist Council and Cardinal Augustin Bea, President of the Vatican Secretariat for Christian Unity. This project was nearly still-born. Difficulties arose from both sides. The Methodists were chary about agreeing to be joint publishers,[4] but not about a preface from Bishop Odd Hagen. The Vatican had no difficulties about the joint publication: its problem was about the text of Cardinal Bea's preface.

In outline the story is as follows. After hearing about John Wesley's *Letter to a Roman Catholic,* written in Dublin in 1749, at the meeting of the World Methodist Council in London in August 1966, I wrote to a staff member whom I knew at the Secretariat for Promoting Christian Unity suggesting a new edition with prefaces from Cardinal Bea and Bishop Hagen and offering to act as editor. No reply came until mid November but with the reply came the text itself of the Cardinal's preface and the news that a copy had already been forwarded to Bishop Hagen. I thought this was indecently hasty. I had expected a preliminary letter of agreement in general to which I might reply, explaining the purpose of the edition more fully and submitting a draft preface for the Cardinal. My negative reaction was all the greater because the Cardinal's preface in my opinion was 'quite unsuitable'.

Unfortunately, on 22 November, I replied with a letter which was not diplomatic enough: I stated openly that 'The Cardinal's preface will have to be completely redone ... by someone with some knowledge of the spirit and theology of Methodism.' Thankfully this letter did not kill the project. The reply described it as a 'negative and harsh reaction' which 'might have compromised the entire worthwhile project' but added that it might be possible to save the situation if I forwarded 'suggestions for the improvement of the Cardinal's preface ... but using the Cardinal's text as a basis'. I saw no future in that and decided to let the matter drop for the moment. So during the following months, while I was teaching in St Paul's University, Ottawa, I myself drafted a text of the Cardinal's preface and 'hoping it may be possible to forget the things that are behind' forwarded it to Rome in April 1967. With one slight change my text was accepted, the Cardinal sent thanks for my 'cooperation – and patience', the publication went ahead, appearing in 1968 and shortly afterwards I was appointed a member of the Methodist/Roman Catholic International Commission.

To end this chapter with another happy memory: the Maynooth Summer School was in an important agent of aggiornamento here in Ireland in the 1960s. When invited in 1965 to contribute a paper on 'The Church in Modern Theology', I took as my subject 'The Fourth Book of Calvin's *Institutes*' and in the course of my paper quoted Calvin's criticism of the Catholic 'priestlings' to the effect that

> They gradually began to make innumerable masses in every corner of the churches and to drag the people hither and thither, when they should have come together in one assembly to recognise the mystery of their unity.

To my surprise the overwhelmingly clerical audience greeted this quotation with spontaneous applause: concelebration of the eucharist was then, in 1965, relatively if not entirely new here in Ireland. Calvin will have been pleased.

CHAPTER SEVEN

Catholic Memories
Part II: Post 1970

If in retrospect the first part of my ecumenical ministry / apostolate can be dated precisely to 9 March 1960 when I gave a Milltown Park Public Lecture on The Movement for Christian Unity, the second part as it happens can also be dated exactly. It began ten years later on 15 April 1970. That was the day the volume *Irish Anglicanism 1869-1969* which I had edited was presented to the Church of Ireland in the person of its Primate, Archbishop George Simms of Armagh.

It was a splendid occasion but the Catholic bishops, by contrast with their Church of Ireland confrères and other dignitaries of church and state, were conspicuous by their absence. Despite special approaches from the publisher, Cardinal Conway declined to be present. Eventually Bishop Birch of Ossory attended to represent the Catholic hierarchy and his presence tempted me, when replying to the toast of the editor, to make the unscripted remark: 'what a heavy responsibililty!' The addition to the text was noted by the *Irish Press* journalist, Mr T. P. O'Mahony who phoned it in immediately to his newsroom and the paper included it the following morning.

Archbishop McQuaid, however, in whose diocese the presentation was taking place, had not been entirely negative. The presentation was planned to begin with an interdenominational service in the chapel of Gonzaga College. The archbishop had asked the Jesuit Provincial Superior, Fr Cecil McGarry, to let him see the Order of Service in advance and he had made one change. The service was to open with the prayer well-known to most Protestants: 'O God ... give us grace seriously to lay to heart the great dangers we are in by our unhappy divisions.' The archbishop insisted that this first petition be altered to read instead: 'seriously to lay to heart the prayer of our divine Saviour that his true followers should be one'. Otherwise, however, he had acquiesced; he had confidence in Fr McGarry as provincial and as special preacher for the occasion.

The service raised two other problems. Some Protestants had misgivings about the proposed use of incense They had acqui- esced however when we pointed out that it was the Bible which it was proposed to incense and that this incensation of the Bible at the beginning of each session of Vatican II had greatly im- pressed the Protestant observers . Fr Romould Dodd OP, how- ever, was not open to persuasion. His involvement that evening was as a Radio Telefis Éireann Religious Affairs producer. RTÉ were televising the service for transmission live from Dublin and for transmission later in the evening from Belfast by UTV. Fr Dodd's plan, I discovered, was to make a short introduction and then let the service go through without any commentary, however discreet. I thought this less than satisfactory for such an unfamiliar service in such unusual circumstances but my com- plaints were not heard and later, in fact, I was officially in- formed that 'the programme was very well received by the vast majority of our viewers'.

At a distance now of some thirty years, I have to ask myself once again was all this another instance of 'Nero fiddling while Rome burnt' – while Northern Ireland burned? On the following day the famous Bannside by-election took place: Ian Paisley un- seated Terence O'Neill, heralding a right-wing Protestant back- lash against reforms. And in the South, after a few weeks the drama of the Arms Crisis and Arms Trial would begin to unfold; and significantly, perhaps, cabinet ministers, Jim Gibbons and Charles Haughey, had cancelled at a late stage their attendance on 15 April. At the time, however, I saw *Irish Anglicanism* as an- other worthwhile venture in the promotion of Christian Unity in general, in particular in the promotion of Catholic-Protestant, Nationalist-Unionist and North-South co-operation in Ireland. It is comforting now in hindsight to know that it was no mere one- off event, however significant, that it led, among other things, to the establishment of the Irish School of Ecumenics

The launching of the Irish School of Ecumenics (ISE) and the launching of *Irish Anglicanism* are indeed so closely related that the compiler of 'Some Notable Events in the Catholic Life of Ireland in 1970', for the 1971 issue of the *Irish Catholic Directory*,

conflated the two. There is no entry for 9 November when ISE
was formally inaugurated but that for 15 April reads mislead-
ingly as follows:

> An Ecumenical Service was held in Gonzaga College, Dublin
> to day to launch the new school of Ecumenics.

Much of the groundwork had, of course, been done in the course
of the previous year. Once *Irish Anglicanism* had been handed to
the publisher in September 1969, I had begun to put on paper the
ideas about ecumenical education which had been crystallising
in my mind since 1960. These, under the title 'Ecumenics: What
and Why?', I had shared with my Jesuit superiors and colleagues. With their approval I had approached leading members
of the other churches and, because these had come to know me
and trust me, they were positive. From a Catholic point of view,
however, it was the attitude of our Archbishop of Dublin which
was crucial. By May the provincial, Fr McGarry, was confident
of his acquiescence and on 22 May he felt able to write to the
President of the Episcopal Conference, Cardinal Conway, and to
the Secretary of the Episcopal Commission on Ecumenism,
Bishop Ahern, informing them of the project. On the 28 May a
press conference followed.

When the formal inauguration of ISE took place on 9
November the three members of the Catholic Episcopal Commission on Ecumenism were conspicuous by their presence, not
by their absence as at the launch of *Irish Anglicanism*. On this occasion it was the Presbyterian Moderator who felt unable to be
present. The inaugural lecture was being given by the General
Secretary of the World Council of Churches which at this time
was coming under increasing criticism not only for its relations
with Rome but also because of its alleged 'support for terrorists'.
These criticisms were finding a strong echo in the Presbyterian
Church in Ireland; its membership of WCC was felt to be at risk
and so, despite his personal commitment to ecumenism, the
Moderator, my friend Principal J. L. M. Haire found it necessary
to excuse himself.

The first major crisis in the life of ISE had occurred even before
its inauguration. The Irish Flour Millers' Association, having
agreed to fund the operation, felt obliged to withdraw. Among
those who then rallied to my emergency appeal was Fr Linus J.

Ryan, then Carmelite provincial who sent a very generous cheque and my friend Fr John Mulligan SJ who as a result of his late mother's will had funds to distribute for good causes at his discretion. This bequest enabled us to buy and refurbish 20 Pembroke Park as a student hostel and specialist library. We called it Bea House after the Jesuit Cardinal who had piloted the *Decree on Ecumenism* through Vatican II. My own Jesuit community gave us office space and access to their library. The Jesuit Director of the nearby College of Industrial Relations, Fr John Brady, gave us the use of a classroom. And the Jesuit provincial later provided substantial funding. So did the Flour Millers' Association, but only as a one-off grant.

ISE's life and work continued to be bedevilled by financial problems until recently, when the Higher Education Authority began to provide core funding through Trinity College Dublin. But among my happy 'Catholic Memories' are those of lay people like Dr J. F. Dempsey, previously of Aer Lingus, who gave sterling service in the early years as ISE Trustee and Chairman of the Finance and Fundraising Committee. It was the official negativity of the Catholic Church which was most discouraging. This came to a climax in the context of the International Consultation on Mixed Marriage.

In a long radio interview which I did with Kevin O'Kelly for his 'Addendum' programme on 21 April 1980, reflecting on my years in ISE, I openly acknowledged our part in the breakdown of relations and of trust with the Catholic hierarchy, and I do so here again. We had seriously misjudged the mood and mind of the Catholic hierarchy on the subject of mixed marriages; we hadn't realised that they were even more uneasy and fearful about the subject than we knew they were; according to the basic rules of dialogue we should, therefore, have been even more sensitive to their feelings than we were – and so we could have been but failed to be.

In the beginning, to ensure good communication, we had invited the Secretary of the Episcopal Commission on Ecumenism, then Bishop Cahal Daly, to be a member of ISE's Academic Council and also of its Executive Board. He had kindly accepted but unfortunately, in sending his apologies for the May 1972 meeting of Board, he asked to be excused from both Council and

Board because of his numerous commitments. One unhappy result was that when I wrote in July 1973 to inform him about the International Consultation on Mixed Marriage which was planned for 2-6 September the following year, he seemed to be taken aback. He misread the dates; he thought the Consultation was scheduled for September 1973 and upraided me for not consulting with his Episcopal Commission.

What ensued was a serious ecumenical crisis: the authenticity and integrity of ISE as an ecumenical institution was at stake. This, however, is not the place to tell the painful story nor am I the appropriate person to attempt to do so objectively. Eventually the Consultation was in many respects a notable success but this success and the publicity accompanying it only aggravated our relationship with the Catholic hierarchy. It reached its nadir in a stormy meeting of the Advisory Committee on Ecumenism, of which I was a member, on 13 February 1975. A resolution was before the meeting. It criticised very negatively a report which had just appeared on the Mixed Marriage Consultation. The resolution, however, was not adopted, was finally not put to a vote for technical reasons of procedure; and the meeting broke up in confusion.

Unfortunately, the situation of ISE in its early years was made still worse by the attitude of Archbishop Dermot Ryan of Dublin. As UCD Professor he had in the beginning been a member of Council and the Council had appointed Church of Ireland Bishop John Armstrong and Mr Eoin McCarthy to represent us at his episcopal ordination in Rome on 13 February, 1972. The archbishop's first reaction in July 1973 to news of the Consultation on Mixed Marriage was positive. In his letter of reply he noted that the Consultation would also consider interfaith marriages and added encouragingly that 'it is important that our own problems concerning mixed marriages in the narrower sense should be seen in a broader context'. And he had sent some of his priests as students to ISE.

However, the archbishop's attitude to ISE was soon to change and to remain changed. When in December 1973 he and the other church leaders received copies of the Consultation programme, he replied resenting the fact that as Archbishop of Dublin he had not previously been consulted. And he did not hesitate to write on 5 January 1974:

I must therefore require that your programme be re-arranged to make places in both the private and public sessions for the presentation of the viewpoints of persons with a genuine pastoral experience in this country.

At that stage, as I wrote in reply on 11 January, relatively little had as yet been done about participation in the Consultation. The archbishop's interest and concern gave us, I suggested, grounds for hope that the insights and experience of Dublin Catholic clergy would be available to the Consultation by their presence. The programme itself, I also pointed out, had not yet been finalised. In particular an 'inter-specialist forum' on 'The Future of Interchurch Marriages in Ireland' had not as yet been arranged. Monsignor Sheehy of the Dublin Chancellery was, I suggested, an obvious person to invite for this and the archbishop would, I hoped, encourage the monsignor to accept the school's invitation.

These hopes were in vain. In a letter of 3 August Archbishop Ryan notified me of his intention not to be present at the Consultation and complained that I had not previously informed him that we were inviting Bishop Butler, Catholic member of the Anglican-Roman Catholic International Commission, to give a public lecture in the autumn on 'A Decade of Ecumenism'. In November he wrote 'to register my strong disapproval' of the way he presumed (without previous enquiry from the organisers) eucharistic hospitality had been encouraged during the Consultation.

In succeeding years he more than once complained to me that ISE was a Protestant rather than an ecumenical institute. He made no secret of his view that ecumenism in Ireland was far too preoccupied with Northern Ireland and with the issue of mixed marriages. He was a very forceful personality. On Cardinal Conway's death in 1977, he took over the co-chairmanship of the InterChurch Ballymascanlon Talks but held on to it until his call to Rome in 1984 instead of yielding it, as might have been expected, to Archbishop Ó Fiaich when in late 1977 the latter was appointed to Armagh and elected to Presidency of the Episcopal Conference.[1]

---

1. Cardinal Ó Fiaich shared with Dr Eric Gallagher (so the latter told me in a conversation on 18 March 1978) the fact that he was hurt by this, all the more so as Ballymascanlon was in his own diocese.

Despite all this official negativity from the Catholic hierarchy, ISE managed to retain its buoyancy and, among other things, an International Consultation on Human Rights was planned and took place from 30 November to 4 December 1978 in celebration of the 30th anniversary of the UN Declaration of Human Rights. This was another considerable success and at the end I made the surprising announcement that I proposed to retire in 1980.

The thought of retirement had come to my mind for the first time during evening prayer in the Jesuit Community of Marquette University in the USA on Saturday 15 January 1977. I had stopped off there on my way to St Paul-Minneapolis where I was to fulfil a number of Unity Week engagements. My main reason was not that the conflict in Northern Ireland was only getting worse. ISE was not founded precisely to solve the Northern Ireland conflict. In ISE the whole wide world was our parish. But was it because of our difficult relationship with the Catholic hierarchy? Did I believe that I personally was the problem and that my going would ease relationships? I don't think I was the problem and the experience of my successors showed that this was not quite the case; the problem was ecumenism itself and the reluctance of the hierarchy to share power. ISE survived the opposition of the Catholic hierarchy firstly because, as Director, I was no mere individual but a Jesuit fully supported by my superiors. It survived secondly because it was an interdenominational institution. However my resignation was, I now think, influenced more than I was willing to admit at the time by the attitude of the Catholic hierarchy. In the late 1970s the situation was easing somewhat. Bishop Cahal Daly paid us a formal friendly visit in April 1977, as did Cardinal Willebrands of the Vatican Secretariat for Promoting Christian Unity in May 1978. It remains that the main reason for my retirement was a conviction that ISE would be unable to develop properly and flourish if it continued to be dependent on the person who was largely responsible for its beginnings and first decade.

The sabbatical which followed, thanks to the generosity of ISE, I have referred to in a previous chapter as 'a gloriously exhilarating experience'. It was a travelling sabbatical. I stayed in exotic places. I walked on the Great Wall of China; I recited the Creed without the *filioque* when concelebrating Mass on the island of Syros. But the two highlights of the year were undoubtedly my visit to Mount Athos and my stay in China; two later chapters attempt to convey something of those experiences.

As noted in chapter two, what happened as a result of my sabbatical year was the establishment in Belfast of the Columbanus Community of Reconciliation. My expectation had been that, with French and English, I might be useful in Africa teaching ecumenical theology for a period of years. My lack of experience of the African scene would have been a major handicap in the beginning, but opportunities did open up especially with the new Institute of Theology about to start in Port Harcourt. The idea, however, of devoting myself to an attempt to establish in Northern Ireland some sort of interdenominational religious community, not unlike Taizé, came to me out of the blue in the middle of a thirty-day retreat which I did in the little Indian village of Sitagarha near Hazaribagh, in north-East India. In fact, as I discovered later, it didn't come altogether out of the blue. It had been in my mind in 1969 as is clear from the last chapter and last page of *Irish Anglicanism*. It had disappeared from my consciousness in the seventies, emerging as a complete new idea in February 1981. After the retreat, the idea grew on me and seemed good to some, if not to all of the Jesuit friends whom I consulted. In particular, it commended itself to my Provincial Superior ,Fr Joseph Dargan, who on my return home in the summer of 1981 suggested that I carry out a feasibility study.

The attitude of the Vatican authorities, and especially of the Irish Catholic bishops with whom I had clashed in the 70s, would obviously be crucial if such an initiative were to get off the ground. To my surprise they were all here at home and in Rome quite positive, especially Cardinal Tomás Ó Fiaich of Armagh and Cardinal Willebrands of the Vatican Council for Promoting Christian Unity. They were of course understandably guarded and cautionary on the question of eucharistic sharing. The attitude of Bishop Cahal Daly became particularly crucial. I had clashed with him in the context of the Interchurch Marriage Consultation. We had decided to locate our experiment in Belfast and he had now been transferred there as Bishop of Down and Connor. He was slow in responding to my letter but his eventual reply gave us a warm welcome to his diocese.

Prayer in common was an essential part of our community life in the Columbanus Community of Reconcilation. We met for prayer morning and evening – and at midday if we happened to be at home. We also celebrated the eucharist together every day except Sunday, though attendance was optional and we refrained from eucharistic sharing. On the strength of this regime of common prayer, we lived together as Catholics and Protestants a life of unity, simplicity and peace. We also ran a small centre in our own premises where quiet days of prayer were held and occasional lectures on issues of unity, justice and peace. We also helped outside the house to service the work of other agencies. Our life together we saw as offering a practical challenge to the sectarianism, injustice and violence prevalent all around us and as offering much needed encouragement to whose already committed to reconciliation.

When the six of us who were to be the founding members (along with a seventh who would arrive later) came together in Belfast on 15 September 1981, the house which was to be ours wasn't yet ready for occupation. In the meantime we stayed with friends. The Christian Brothers on Somerton Road were my hosts, and when I visited the parish priest who lived opposite he unhesitatingly gave me a key to his house and invited me to use it whenever I wished. With this generous gesture there began for me what was to be a very happy decade of my life. I remembered Bishop Mageean's letter of commendation when my pamphlet *Towards Christian Unity* appeared away back in 1960.

Since the 1980s my relationship with the Catholic hierarchy has been different: no longer uneasy as it had been during the 60s and 70s. Their controversial decision to transfer the celebration of the Feast of the Ascension from the traditional Thursday to the following Sunday did trouble me: it was unilateral without consultation with the Church of Ireland who continue as before and without consultation with the Catholic people who, like their English and Welsh counterparts, might well have disagreed. Despite correspondence with a number of the bishops immediately concerned, the decision was unfortunately not – so far – reversed.

When in 1993, after ten years, I decided to withdraw from membership of the Columbanus Community I retained my role

as Trustee. This eventually involved me in facing a painful decision about its closure which came in September 2002. The early,
premature death of an institution can be as painful as that of an
individual. CCR had begun formally on 15 September 1983; I
had begun working on the project in 1981.

Why this early death? The immediate reasons were decline in
residential membership and decline in financial support. In recent years, fewer individuals seemed attracted by residential
membership and those who did volunteer stayed for shorter
and shorter periods. This resulted in a crisis of identity.
Columbanus no longer had a good memory. There was less interest in, less knowledge and appreciation of its origins, its history,
its ethos. There was no strong living tradition which could be
the source of authentic development.

This crisis of identity was, however, on its way to being resolved. There was an emerging agreement. It was generally
agreed that the future for Columbanus was as a Centre more
than as a Community. This agreement found expression in the
way the renovation of the premises at 683 Antrim Road was
planned. But hardly had this work of renovation been completed
than it emerged that there was no money left to enable
Columbanus to face the future as a Centre. Our financial appeal
had only been a very partial success.

The more remote reasons are many: among others, the decline in vocations to religious orders both Anglican and Catholic;
the decline in volunteering which has hit most voluntary
organisations, secular as well as religious; the decline in interest
in ecumenism which results logically from the decline in a
church-centred spirituality; a growing fatigue with projects of
reconciliation which of their nature take years and years; a
growing fatigue with Northern Ireland in particular, and last
but not least, changes in the funding policies and practices of
official institutions such as the Community Relations Council in
Northern Ireland.

The logic which in 1980 decided my retirement from ISE after
ten years also decided my retirement from membership of
Columbanus after a decade: it too needed to stand on its own
feet. Besides, in 1993 I was celebrating my 70th birthday, a climacteric suggesting withdrawal from active service, especially

as a Festschrift in my honour was published on the occasion, and all four church leaders including Cardinal Daly came from Northern Ireland to launch the volume at TCD, giving me very generously the 'Euge, Euge. Well done, Well Done' of the Parable of the Talents (cf Mt 25: 21, 22). A photograph of that memorable occasion features of course among those that adorn the walls of my study bedroom.

Back in Dublin since then and living at Milltown Park, most of my engagements have in fact come from the other churches, but I have given a few directed retreats to the priests of the Armagh diocese and preached Unity Week sermons in Holy Cross Church Dundrum and in St Michael's Dúnlaoire. Against the background of my uneasy relationship with the Catholic hierarchy during the 60s and 70s it was a particular consolation when in 1998 Archbishop Brady and the other church leaders contributed generous prefaces for my collection of essays, *Christian Unity: An Ecumenical Second Spring?*, and when the President of the Pontifical Commission for Christian Unity, Cardinal Cassidy, came from Rome to launch the book both in Belfast and in Dublin. In July of the following year, I had the great joy of celebrating the eucharist at an interdenominational gathering of the members and friends of the Columbanus Community and, with due permission, inviting all who wished to come to communion. The occasion was the retirement from Leadership of Sr Roisin Hannaway, SSL. What she and I and all of us had, in the words of St Luke (22:15), 'longed and longed for' was such eucharistic hospitality on special occasions as a foretaste of the banquet of heaven to encourage us on our way.

CHAPTER EIGHT

Orthodox / Mount Athos Memories

Introduction

'There can be no fulfillment of the divine purpose in any scheme of reunion which does not ultimately include the great Latin Church of the West, with whom our history has been so closely associated in the past, and to which we are still bound by very many ties of common faith and tradition.'

All of us in the West, Anglicans, Catholics and Protestants need to convince ourselves that this remarkable, historic statement by the Lambeth Conference of 1908 applies also to the churches of the East. We do perhaps agree in principle that there can be no fulfillment of the divine purpose in any scheme of reunion which does not ultimately include the great churches of the East but, if so, our assent is more notional than real. The long estrangement between West and East has left us in the West ignorant and impoverished, very vulnerable to a narrow, exclusively Western view of Catholicism. So westernised and isolated have we become that we have largely forgotten that the Christian religion is in origin an Eastern religion and that the church, to be one, must, in the words of Pope John Paul II, 'breathe with both its lungs'.

My two main experiences of Orthodoxy were a week's stay, during the millennium year, at the Monastery of St John the Baptist in Essex, a joint monastery of Orthodox monks and nuns, and a three or four day visit to the independent monastic republic of Mount Athos in Greece in 1980. The former was a more positive experience. I was made very welcome. I was able to participate in all the offices and assist at the eucharist, though of course without receiving communion, and to share meals with the community in their dining room. The latter was more negative than positive. It is not, however, either unfair or unecumenical to include here my diary account of the visit to Mount Athos.

It reveals something of the ancient antipathy between Catholics and Orthodox which recent events since the fall of the Berlin Wall show not to have abated but rather intensified. And relations between the Orthodox and the World Council of Churches of the World are also poor. My stay in the Monastery of St John the Baptist was a sign of hope. My stay on Mount Athos shows that to hope is indeed to hope against hope.

Mount Athos

An advertisement for Hugh Leonard's play, *Da*, is one of the first things I notice in Aristotle Square on my arrival here this evening (30 September 1980). I'm simply passing through Salonica, coming from the Meteora monasteries of Thessaly and going on tomorrow to the Orthodox monasteries of Mount Athos, the most eastern of the three peninsulas jutting out from the coast of Macedonia in northern Greece.

At midday I had an appointment to see Metropolitan Rodopoulos at the university, where he is Professor of Canon Law. He speaks excellent English and entertained me most hospitably to lunch afterwards on the balcony of his apartment overlooking the bay. He is a very sympathetic supporter of the ecumenical movement and served as a member of the Academic Council of the Irish School of Ecumenics in its early years, but he doesn't think progress in the new Orthodox-Roman Catholic dialogue will be dramatic. If I understood him right, he also seems to think that the monks on Mount Athos will not allow me to join them, not only for the Eucharist but for any of their services. I find this incredible, even for Mount Athos.

With all our talk, it is 4.30 pm before we realise it and the Metropolitan very kindly drives me to the 5.30 pm bus for Ouranoupolis: this is a seaside village at the top of the south side of the Mount Athos peninsula and it is from here you take the boat to the port of entry. The road to Ouranoupolis takes us over the mountains, past wayside shrines and beehives and through the village of Stagira, birthplace of Aristotle, but it is dark by then. About 8.00 pm, as we near our destination and most of the other passengers have got off, a friendly young man engages me in conversation. He wonders – in broken German – if I also am going to visit the Holy Mountain. He is a Greek – his name is

Rallis – and when we arrive I have no difficulty with his help in getting lodgings for the night.

Our fellow-lodgers include two Orthodox priests and a young German named Tom, who is also going to Mount Athos. When we have settled into our rooms, Rallis, Tom and I go out to share a bottle of wine. Rallis lives near Salonica and has just finished his studies as a mechanical engineer. He has friends on Mount Athos and will stay a week or ten days. Greeks don't need special permits as we do, nor are they limited to the ordinary four-day stay. His family is very religious; he himself does not keep the regular Friday fast but he does keep the Lenten fast. Tom is from Hamburg and begins university in the autumn. His family background is Protestant, but he has been an atheist and is now becoming an Orthodox Christian in the Russian Church in Exile. Tom is a very serious young man.

The boat for Dafni, which is the name of the port of entry to Mount Athos, isn't due to depart until 9.45 am. Before that Rallis, Tom and I explore the little seaside village of Ouranoupolis, have morning coffee and buy ourselves provisions for the lean days ahead, cheese and chocolate and fruit.

Examining the map when we get on board, I see that the port of Dafni where we are heading is over half-way down the southern coast and that the whole peninsula is about twenty-five miles long and seven miles wide. Looking around at my fellow passengers, I see that one of the monks with his different headgear is quite obviously Russian and I approach him. He speaks English but better French and is quite willing to talk. He belongs to the Russian Church in Exile and lives in a monastery in the south of France. He has previously spent a year here on Mount Athos but found the regime too hard and is now going back to visit friends.

There are twenty monasteries, he explains, and they have parcelled out the whole peninsula between them. No new monasteries can be established, only *sketes* or dependent monastic institutions. We pass the monastery of Panteleimon and he speaks of the Russian influence on Mount Athos before the Revolution, when this monastery numbered some two thousand monks. It still is, he says, a Russian monastery, but has only a handful of monks. There are two other non-Greek monasteries: one Serbian and the other Bulgarian.

About midday we all disembark at Dafni and climb aboard a bus which takes us slowly and dangerously up the steep, narrow dirt road to the village of Karies. This is the 'administrative capital' of Mount Athos, and the Roman Catholic Church had a small school here from 1636-41. All of us non-Greeks have now to present ourselves at the police station, but it is closed for lunch. There is a restaurant of sorts where we repair for a bite to eat, and afterwards I buy a useful map giving the location of all the monasteries and the distance in kilometres and walking hours, between them. By then the police station is open; it is staffed for the monks by the Greek police. Here my permit from the Ministry of Foreign Affairs in Athens is scrutinised and exchanged for another document. This I bring along to the monastic GHQ, where I receive my *diamoneterion*, the visa which everyone needs and which calls on the individual monasteries to give me hospitality for the five days I have requested. Rallis, Tom and I now say goodbye because we are going to different monasteries, and I set out on my own path to Stavronikita.

It was Metropolitan Rodopoulos who suggested Stavronikita; the Abbot had studied at Paris and would be good to meet. This monastery is situated on the northern coast of the peninsula, so the walk there has to be downhill and, according to the map, I should make it in an hour and a half. The prospect therefore is not too daunting – some journeys on Mount Athos take four hours and more – but I'm carrying too much in my shoulder bag, the afternoon sun is beating down fiercely, the signposting is not too clear, and being alone I begin to be anxious. Am I really going in the right direction on the right path? If I've taken a wrong turn and am going astray and don't arrive before sunset when the monasteries close up, what on earth am I going to do for the night? Eventually, to my great relief, I see below a tower which must be Stavronikita.

The guestmaster greets me silently, motions me to take a seat and disappears for a moment to return with a square of Turkish delight and a glass of water. Then he asks for my *diamoneterion* and enters all the details in the guestbook. Shortly afterwards two young Greeks arrive and he does likewise but then he goes off, bringing the Greeks with him, and I am left on my own in the waiting room, wondering what's going on.

Since my arrival, however, the *simantron*, the wooden sound-ing-board which summons the monks to prayer, is being struck, and so I am forced very reluctantly to the conclusion that vespers are on and that Metropolitan Rodopoulos was right: as a non-Orthodox I am barred. The conclusion is only too true. Forty-five minutes later the guestmaster returns and invites me with him to the church, where now the lights are being extinguished and the departing worshippers are venerating the icons. I stand in silent prayer, but I do not join in the veneration; my resentment doesn't allow me. Later I shall very much regret this.

It is now 5.00 pm and supper follows with the monks, a privilege which, as I shall discover, not every monastery on Mount Athos grants to its guests. The meal is excellent, and from the glances I can manage around the refectory as we eat in silence, I gather that there are sixteen monks present; but, very puzzlingly, there is not one old man among them. After supper the guestmaster shows the two Greeks and myself to our room which is three flights up, overlooking the sea and with five beds. He tells me that the Abbot is away but that another monk who speaks English will see me tomorrow morning after lunch about 9.30 am (*sic*). There is still light and the doors are not closed so I wander outside to calm my troubled spirits in the cool of the evening. At 6.30 pm I am back in the house. Oil lamps are now lighting in the corridors. I light the one in our dormitory and sit and try to think and write, but I am still upset when I go to bed some time later.

We were called at 2.45 this morning but I had to presume the call was only for my Orthodox companions who could join the monks for the office. When I emerge about 7.00 am the church is locked. Later I find out that all the monastery churches on Mount Athos are closed between offices for security reasons; icons have been stolen.

At my request, the guestmaster now opens the church but remains inside with me and when I go to sit down, he indicates that we should be leaving. He then offers the two Greeks and myself a coffee in his waiting room and we get into conversation. One of the Greeks is a mathematics teacher, the other an artist of some sort; both are from Athens. They speak English fairly well and try to explain to me in friendly fashion why I cannot join in prayer with the monks: the Orthodox have the truth and Catholics are in error. When I suggest that in this matter of ecumenism, Mount Athos may be out of step with the rest of the Orthodox world, one of them says that he believes Demetrios, the Patriarch of Constantinople, to be in the pay of the Freemasons.

From 8.00 am I sit quietly at the open window of our dormitory, looking out to sea, listening to the waves breaking gently on the rocks below, preparing questions for my session later with the English-speaking monk and reviewing my plans for the day. To my left I can see the monastery of Pantokratoros, but I decide now to visit Iviron instead. This is out of sight to my right. It is the second-oldest monastery on Mount Athos, celebrating this year its foundation in Georgia just a millennium ago, in 980. Last summer I had a memorable few days in Tbilisi and a most interesting audience with the Orthodox Patriarch there. I decide to go to Iviron in order to pray for the Church in Georgia.

The meal at 9.30 am, which we are allowed again to take with the monks, is definitely lunch and a very good lunch, but one of the servers admonished me for sitting with my legs crossed under the table. Afterwards I sit outside and chat with the English-speaking monk, a Greek whose name is Father Simeon and who came here from Athens in 1974.

According to my watch it is 10.45 am on 3 October but for him it is 4.45 pm on 20 September. They still follow the Julian calendar (as do all the monasteries except one) and for them sunset is midnight. This means that the monks retired last night at 12.30 am (6.30 pm by me), got up at 7.00 am (1.00 am by me), had lunch at 3.30 pm (9.30 am by me) and, were this not Friday, would have supper this evening at 11.00 pm (5 pm by me). On Mondays, Wednesdays and Fridays they take only one meal in the day.

At present, I gather from Father Simeon, there are twenty monks in the monastery, four of them priests. There are no elderly monks because the monastery had been closed and re-opened only in 1968 to begin a new chapter in its history; it changed from being ideorrhythmic to being coenobitic. The coenobitic style of monastic life is stricter, with greater emphasis on community; the ideorrhythmic monks live a more independent, individualistic life. Fifteen of the monasteries are now coenobitic and the total monastic population numbers between 1,400 and 1,500.

They do not allow other non-Orthodox Christians to be in church with them during the offices, because we would be mere spectators and because 'the Holy Fathers' forbid it; we may, however, stay in the porch. Before taking my leave of Father Simeon and thanking him, I tell him that I also am a monk, a religious. 'But where,' he asks, 'is your habit?' An Orthodox monk, no matter what work he is at, never seems to leave aside his habit.

It's already about midday by my watch when I say goodbye to Stavronikita and set out on the path along the cliffs towards Iviron which, according to the map, I should reach in less than an hour. Unfortunately, I lose my way and spend an anxious quarter of an hour moving blindly through thick vegetation in what I hope is the right direction. At last I arrive safely and have the added pleasure of a brief meeting with Rallis who is about to leave, but the guesthouse, I find, is closed until 4.00 pm. Meantime the water is tempting and a swim would be very welcome but the monks, I gather, are forbidden to go in, so I refrain and instead look around and take a rest in the shade.

Iviron seems at first sight to be a much bigger establishment than Stavronikita but less well maintained. You come up from the pier through an entrance gate, which has the date – 1867 – painted overhead, into a large quadrangle. In the centre of this there are three churches to the left and buildings to the right, which later I am able to identify as the library and a former refectory. All around there are stairways which presumably lead to the private apartments of the monks – this is an ideorrhythmic monastery. On the north side is the guesthouse. Although somewhat dilapidated in appearance, Iviron is certainly an impressive place.

By the time the *simantron* sounds for vespers I am fully rested and recovered from my walk along the cliffs, and I decide to go into the church and see if I shall be allowed to stay for the office. There is no difficulty discovering which of the three churches is to be used. I join the monks there and happily none of them objects to my presence. At the end I join with them in venerating the icons. Afterwards the guesthouse opens and other visitors arrive. The guestmaster offers us an ouzo with turkish delight and water; doesn't ask for our *diamoneterion* but invites us very casually to enter the details ourselves in the guestbook, and then shows us to the dormitories. The toilet facilities are very primitive indeed.

Supper is at 5.00 pm and when all the visitors gather together we turn out to be a very motley group: a Greek Orthodox priest (who has spent eight years in Melbourne but speaks only very broken English) with a few of his parishioners, three Germans, two Austrians and an American from Cleveland who is Orthodox and can speak Greek. We are eating on our own in the guesthouse and not with the monks, presumably because in idiorrhythmic monasteries the monks do not eat together in a common refectory. The fare is barely tolerable, even with the glass of retsina which we have to wash it down, and I shall later have to dip into the provisions bought at Ouranoupolis. After supper I ask to be called at 5.00 am in order to attend the later part of the morning office, and wander around outside again, chatting with some of the other guests. Before too long, however, I retire upstairs to the dormitory. There I read by lamplight and go over in memory the happy events of my visit last year to Georgia. And last thing before going to bed I review my plans for tomorrow. Dionisiou, which I am visiting next, is on the south side of the peninsula. To get there from Iviron which is on the north side I have to walk up to Karies, the 'administrative capital', in time to catch the bus from Dafni where I can get a boat for Dionisiou. This means an early start tomorrow.

The church is all dark when I come down this morning but with the help of my torch I discover the Greeks and the American at the back and I sit with them until the chanting of the office is over. Neither they nor the monks resent my presence but I begin to wonder if this tolerance is due to conviction or to indifference. At 6.30 coffee is served in the guesthouse and we learn that later in the morning, because it is Saturday, there will be a bus to Karies. This is great news if it can be relied on; it saves me a two-hour uphill walk and it also gives me more time here at Iviron. I decide to risk it and wait for the bus and in the meantime to look around some more.

Four monks are in evidence around the guesthouse, two of them on the younger side, and while I wait I manage to engage one of these in conversation. He speaks English quite well, having spent five years in New York. Until fairly recently he has been a monk at Grigoriou but left it to come here because he found it too strict. In all, he tells me, there are fifteen monks at Iviron and 1867 – the date over the gate – is the date the monastery was rebuilt after one of the fires which seem to have destroyed almost every monastery on Mount Athos at one time or another. While I wait I also succeed in getting into the library. A monk carrying books appears in the quadrangle and allows me to accompany him. The library is well kept and includes among its treasures some relics of the Patriarch of Constantinople, Gregory V, who was hanged by the Turks in 1821. I also catch a glimpse of the monastery making its wine: a young monk in Wellington boots stands in a barrel treading the grapes and keeping his balance by means of a rope hanging from a bar above. He is, of course, wearing his habit!

When the bus for Karies arrives about 10.30 I find that Tom is one of the passengers and, like long-lost friends, we exchange all our news. He is coming from the monastery of Philotheou and feels somewhat deflated. Not only was he not allowed to join the monks at prayer in the church but he couldn't join them for meals in the refectory either. Being an Orthodox aspirant he took this very hard, but for the monks he was still a heretic. Philotheou, he says, has only become coenobitic in recent years and is very strict. The number of monks rose from nine to ninety and has now dropped to forty but only because many have gone to strengthen other monasteries. Tom leaves the bus at Karies but I continue on down to the port of Dafni where I had arrived on Thursday. Here, with a number of other visitors, I take a small boat for Dionisiou which is further on along the coast in the opposite direction from Ouranoupolis. On the way we pass Grigoriou where I plan to stay tomorrow night.

The monastery of Dionisiou rises sheer out of the sea on top of a steep rock and makes a most impressive sight from the boat. It is only a short walk up from the harbour and, when we arrive, we are greeted by the guestmaster with a glass of ouzo as well as the usual turkish delight and water. He is careful, however, to ask us for our diamoneterion and to take down all our particulars before showing us to the dormitories. His English is quite good and I gather from him that there are some forty-five monks, that vespers will be at 9.00 pm (it is now 7.15 pm by the monastery time though only 1.15 pm by my watch) and that my presence would be tolerated in the porch of the church.

While waiting for vespers I stand out over the sea on one of the many balconies which project from the monastery walls and admire the splendid view. Then I go to the church. The resentment I had felt at Stavronikita has now given way to sadness and the sobering realisation that the Roman Catholic Church has much to regret and repent of in its relations with the Orthodox Church. I assist therefore at the office from the porch in a spirit of penance which a passing monk gauchely tries to improve by admonishing me for sitting with my legs crossed. Supper follows immediately but only for the monks. The guests eat separately and later. This seems to me perfectly logical because community meals in monasteries include prayer and spiritual reading. I do not therefore take it as hard as Tom did but it is pushing the policy of apartheid to an extreme. Supper when it comes is excellent and very welcome because I haven't really had a proper meal since lunch yesterday at 9.30 am at Stavronikita. After supper I page through some of the English-language periodicals provided in the guesthouse. To my horror I read that ecumenism is 'a spiritual disease' ... 'totally alien to Orthodoxy', and that Patriarch Demetrious of Constantinople 'speaks the language of the ideology of freemasonry'. I go to bed with a heavy heart. The plan for tomorrow is to leave early to get the boat for Grigoriou.

The church is open and empty when I come down this morning at 6.00 am. Sitting in the porch in calmer mood I think further about the alienation which exists between Eastern and Western Christians; how appropriate it is that Roman Catholics do penance for our misdeeds, especially during the crusades, and how inappropriate it would be for an Irishman to reproach the Orthodox for their long memories. As far as the monks of Mount Athos are concerned, it is quite disconcerting that their anti-ecumenism should be a feature not of a decadent but of a flourishing monasticism. Isolationism would appear to be one important factor. In any case, experience has shown that ecumenical prejudices anywhere can be softened only by contact with other Christians. But has the Roman Catholic Church in Greece the requisite resources? Promising myself to discuss this question with friends in Athens in the next few days, I hurry off down to the harbour to catch the boat which is due at 8.00 am.

It is only a short, twenty-minute run to the monastery of Grigoriou which is further back the coast in the direction of Dafni. On the way I remember the young Iviron monk who told me he had found it too strict here, but it can't, I tell myself, be any grimmer, ecumenically, than Dionisiou was. When we arrive at 8.45 am we climb up the steps from the harbour, pass under a vine trellis in the monastery courtyard and find that the monks are just finishing lunch. Straightaway we are invited to 'second table' and while we eat, the refectory is being set for supper to the accompaniment of chanted prayers.

There is a long interval now between lunch and vespers but it gives me ample opportunity for looking around, for chatting with some of the guests and perhaps some of the monks and for quiet reflection. Besides, I have asked for an appointment with the Abbot to whom I bring greetings from Metropolitan Rodopoulos; it was he who recommended me to visit both Dionisiou and Grigoriou.

Later in the morning as I wander around I manage to engage one of the monks in conversation. As it happens, he is an ex-Roman Catholic from Latin America who came in contact with Orthodoxy in Paris. He is adamant that Christian unity can be achieved only by repentance and a return to the common faith of the first millennium, i.e. only in the Orthodox Church. He considers joint prayer, even the recitation of the Our Father, to be impossible because our classical differences in trinitarian theology mean that our notion of God the Father is quite different. He thinks that Western Christianity has been corrupted by rationalism and materialism.

In the course of the afternoon I reflect that Mount Athos, although a very beautiful and interesting place, is only for the robust – physically, spiritually and ecumenically. The monks are concerned to keep mere tourists out and I share their concern.

Despite their precautions, however, too many visitors seem to have too little real interest in religion. As a result Christianity and monasticism suffer from their association here with religious intolerance – and with primitive plumbing. I share this reflection with one of my fellow-visitors and Dominique agrees with me. He is a university student, French and Roman Catholic. He regrets in particular that the monasteries of Mount Athos, unlike Taizé and other places in Europe, do so little to help the faith of their visitors.

After vespers, during which I sit in the porch of the church, the Abbot receives me. He is very hospitable – I am offered a fig and a coffee – but also very firm. He is happy with the development of monasticism on Mount Athos and thinks that the few remaining ideorrhythmic monasteries will have become coenobitic in five or six years' time. He is less than happy about the development of ecumenism in the Orthodox Church. He emphasises that he is not opposed to all dialogue but only to that form of dialogue which encourages common prayer and the kiss of peace. What is needed in his view is that Roman Catholics – and other Western Christians – repent of their errors, be baptised (*sic*) and so restored to the unity of the church.

Supper follows immediately on this sobering, chilling conversation and the Abbot conducts me very graciously to the refectory where we guests are allowed to eat at the same time as the monks. Afterwards I retire at once to the dormitory. Today's conversations have done no more than put in words what was otherwise conveyed at Dionisiou and also at Stavronikita. But the words, none the less, have had a shattering effect, all the worse because of the Abbot's exquisite courtesy and because he is quite obviously a deeply religious man.

Before taking the boat this morning, my last on Mount Athos, I spend some time again in the porch of the Grigoriou church reflecting on the experiences of the last few days. For myself I am happy and grateful to have had these experiences, however painful and penitential. But Pope John Paul's visit to Constantinople in December 1979 comes to mind and the hope he expressed there and then that the end of the second and the beginning of the third millennium would bring unity between Catholics and Orthodox.

How, I ask myself, can Christian unity ever become a reality by the year 2000 if Orthodox attitudes are as negative as I have been finding them here on Mount Athos? This, I see, is another question I must discuss tomorrow in Salonica. It is time now to take my departure so I venerate the icons – regretting once again my failure to do so at Stavronikita – and walk down to the harbour to catch the boat, first for Dafni and then for Ouranoupolis.

For some strange reason there is the formality of a customs check at Dafni before you leave the Holy Mountain but I am carrying no stolen icons or anything else of an incriminating nature. In conversation on board with other passengers it emerges that not all the monasteries are rigid in the matter of joint worship. The pattern in ideorrhythmic monasteries, in particular in the three non-Greek monasteries, seems to be more relaxed and much as I had experienced it myself at Iviron, but whether from conviction or indifference remains unclear. One of the passengers with whom I chat has left his car at Ouranoupolis and he very kindly offers me a lift to Salonica, which I gladly accept. Hugh Leonard's *Da* is no longer playing but I stroll along the seafront from Aristotle Square to the White Tower and watch the sun go down, and the thought suddenly strikes me that monks of course, engaging in dialogue on the subject of monasticism, would be the most appropriate to improve relations with Mount Athos.

Before leaving Salonica today I have appointments at the university with Metropolitan Rodopoulos and Professor Kalogirou of the Theology Department. They both assure me that Greek Orthodox attitudes in general are not as negative as those of Mount Athos. On the other hand, I also gather that they would not consider 'unity by 2000' to be a very realistic objective. My Roman Catholic friends in Athens with whom I discuss the matter this evening show me the text of a special statement on 'Dialogue with Roman Catholics', issued last April by the Abbots of Mount Athos. It is more outspoken, perhaps, than was Abbot Grigoriou in conversation, but otherwise no different. They admit that people in general are not as extremist in their attitudes as the monks of Mount Athos are, but they insist that anti-ecumenical and anti-Roman Catholic prejudice is widespread and deeply ingrained and must be taken very seriously.

They agree that such prejudice can be overcome only by contact and co-operation, by what Pope John Paul at Constantinople called 'the dialogue of charity'. They also agree that, as far as Mount Athos is concerned, Latin Rite religious and monks would be the most appropriate partners in the dialogue of charity. They very much doubt, however, that the Roman Catholic Church in Greece has by itself the resources to cope at any level with this challenge. The prospect may not be very encouraging but, as I prepare to leave Greece tomorrow, the phrase in the gospels about 'the faith that can move mountains' keeps coming to my mind. This gives me renewed hope. If there is a Christian faith that can move mountains, there is also an ecumenical faith that can move even the Holy Mountain of Mount Athos. We must hope against hope.

Conclusion

And twenty years and more later, it is clear that to hope against hope is really to hope with 'the hope that does not disappoint'(Rom 5:5). Relations between East and West, Catholic-Orthodox relations in particular, may still be poor but my week's stay during the millennium year in the Orthodox Monastery of St John the Baptist near London is only one of the many signs of hope which encourage and enable ecumenists to continue.

CHAPTER NINE

China Memories

What follows is a brief account of some of the religious impressions left by a visit to China in March 1981. A concluding paragraph will indicate some of the significant changes that have since taken place.

The great new fact which I experienced in 1981 was that, after a cruel winter of hardship and suffering, spring was quite definitely in the air again for Christianity in China. My main 'ecumenical' interest, however, concerned the divisions within the Catholic Church. On the one hand there were bishops recognised by Rome but not by the government – 'the underground church' – and on the other hand, there were those bishops who, accepting state registration, were recognised by the government but not by Rome, were members of the Patriotic Association – 'the official church'. If ecumenism is basically a methodology which, *mutatis mutandis*, can be applied in any case of corporate estrangement, it must, I felt, be relevant to the Catholic Church in China.

On each of my three mornings in Beijing I went out by myself to early Mass at the Nan Tang, the seventeenth-century Jesuit church, the Cathedral of the Immaculate Conception, which has been open again since 1971. On the first morning, 18 March, I found to my great surprise that a solemn Requiem Mass in Latin, according to the Tridentine Rite, was taking place with a congregation of about five hundred, for Bishop Francis X. Zhao SJ of Xianxian who had died in prison in 1968, having consecrated six other bishops. The celebrant was Bishop Joseph Zong Huaide of Jinan, president of the Chinese Catholic Patriotic Association. The absolution at the catafalque was given by Bishop Michael Fu Tieshan of Beijing.

On the second morning, the feast of St Joseph, there was a congregation of about two hundred who recited prayers in

Chinese, according to local custom, all during the Mass which, of course, was again celebrated in Latin and according to the Tridentine Rite. The third morning was not a special occasion and the numbers were down to about eighty. On this, as on the previous day, Mass was celebrated successively at the high altar from 5.30 to 7.00 am and there were also some Masses at one of the side altars.

These three early morning Masses were a pure pre-Vatican II experience. It was very moving to hear once again the chants of the Requiem, to see the altar-servers go up at the elevation and hold the corners of the celebrant's chasuble, and to end Mass with 'the last gospel', the reading of the prologue from St John. I was impressed by the fact that a good half of the congregation each morning were men of all ages and that the leader of the prayers was also a man, but young people in their teens were conspicuous by their absence. I was told later in Hong Kong that a government regulation prohibits preaching and the administration of baptism to those under eighteen.

While in Beijing I also succeeded in visiting the tomb of the famous Jesuit missionary, Matteo Ricci, the fourth centenary of whose arrival in China would take place the following year, 1982. The property in which the tomb is located formerly belonged to the Jesuits and then to the Vincentians. It is now in the hands of the Beijing municipality which uses it to run a school for cadres, or party leaders. A visit to the tomb therefore requires a special permit which the Irish ambassador kindly obtained for me. To the right of Ricci is Ferdinand Verbiest, to his left is Adam Schall, both companions of his. In front of each is a large impressive stele with an inscription in Latin and Chinese. All three are enclosed in a small plot surrounded by a railing, and there is now no sign of any other grave. The first blossoms I saw in China were in these grounds, near this little cemetery. I prayed that a second spring was beginning for the Chinese Christianity which these great missionaries had done so much to promote.

Apart from these visits, my stay in Beijing was spent sightseeing – the Forbidden City, The Temple of Heaven, the Great Wall and the tombs of the Ming Dynasty. By a happy coincidence the Ming tomb which we were brought to visit was that of

Wan Li (1573-1619), the emperor who had welcomed Ricci. I did not manage to visit the Dong Tang (St Joseph's), the second Catholic church which was then open in Beijing.

From Beijing our group flew about 550 miles south-west to Xian and stayed there three nights. Xian is one of China's ancient capitals and is associated specially with the Tang dynasty (618-906 CE), considered to be one of the greatest periods in Chinese history. Its achievements include not only the first newspaper and the first true porcelain, exclusively white, but also the creation of the examination system as a means of entering the imperial civil service. Xian is perhaps best known today as the place where Chiang Kai Shek was kidnapped in 1946 and for the archaeological finds of the 1950s and 1970s – a six-thousand-year-old neolithic village and the thousands of clay figures of soldiers and horses found in the tomb of the first emperor of a unified China (246-210 BCE). In the days of the Tang dynasty, Xian was the beginning – or end – of the silk route, and China at that time, it is said, was more open than in the following thousand years. In 1981 foreigners in Xian were an unusual sight, and we attracted enormous attention, but according to the local tourist literature 'thousands of foreign diplomatic envoys, students, clergymen and merchants' lived there under the Tang. These, of course, included Christians.

The coming of Christianity to China in 635, and the welcome it received, is recorded on a famous stele carved in 781 which can be seen today in the Shaanxi Historical Museum at Xian. Unfortunately this Nestorian Christianity, for which there is now a new sympathy, was suppressed by imperial edict in 845 but did not altogether disappear. According to Latourette's *A History of Christian Missions in China*, the marvel is that it survived so long, for two centuries and a half, in what was then 'the mightiest empire on earth', with 'Buddhism at the acme of its vigour'. It is salutary to stand by the nine-foot monument of black limestone and to reflect that Christianity, although, like Buddhism, foreign in origin, has never succeeded in becoming a popular religion in China as Buddhism did.

I was told in Beijing that a Catholic church was open in Xian. On my return to Hong Kong I was able to confirm this information; the cathedral, I gathered, had been open since the previous

Christmas with three priests serving it, one of whom was not a member of the Patriotic Association. During my stay in Xian, however, to my great disappointment I was unable to locate this church. The only reward I had for my efforts was an invitation to his home for an evening meal from a friendly young student who tried to help me. The fact that he and his family felt free to welcome me in this way seemed to be a good indication of the new relaxed atmosphere in China even then and more so now.

Our stay in Xian ended with a visit to the Great Mosque which dates from 742. There are fourteen mosques in Xian for some sixty thousand Muslims. In the country as a whole the number of Muslims is estimated to be between ten and fifty million. They belong to ten different national minorities and are concentrated in western areas: Qinghai, Ningxia, Gansu. During the cultural revolution the Great Mosque in Xian was closed for a year. Muslims in China appear to many to be receiving especially favourable treatment.

From Xian we went due east on a seven-and-a-half-hour train journey to Luoyang, another ancient capital and now a centre of heavy industry. During a short stay we spent a whole morning visiting some of the Lungmen Grottoes which are of great artistic and religious interest. In all there are over a thousand grottoes and some hundred thousand statues of the Buddha, ranging in size from over one inch to fifty-seven feet. They belong to the four-hundred-year period from CE 494 to the end of the Tang dynasty, during which the notorious Empress Wu was a great supporter of Buddhism.

From Luoyang another train journey of over fourteen hours took us to Shanghai which, in the old pre-World War II days, was such an important colonial and Christian centre. Today the concessions belonging to the Western powers have disappeared and Christianity has emerged from the catacombs. During our few days I saw crucifixes and statues of Madonna and Child on sale at the railway station and I attended Mass one morning early in the cathedral at Xujiahui. As in Beijing there was a succession of Masses from 5.30 to 7.00 am, with a congregation of about eighty who seemed, however, to be more elderly and female than the Beijing congregation. It was an ordinary weekday, of course. I gathered that about a thousand go to Mass on

Sundays, that seventeen young people were baptised the previous Christmas and that a Catholic church outside Shanghai re-
opened at the end of 1980. I also gathered that there were five
Protestant churches open, and that these held eleven services at
weekends attended by some fifteen thousand worshippers,
about a quarter of whom were young people.

Our twelve-day trip to China ended with a one-night stay in
Canton, whose Catholic bishop Dominic Tang Yee-ming (Deng
Yiming) SJ, released from prison a short time previously, but not
a member of the Patriotic Association, was very much in the
news at the time. Unfortunately, I was able to admire the mag-
nificent cathedral only from the outside because we were leaving early and it did not open until 7.00 am. My taxi driver, however, smiled, said 'Amen' and blessed himself.

While in China I had lengthy conversations – in English,
French and Latin – with five Catholic priests, two of whom were
not members of the Patriotic Association. I had a formal interview, with the help of an interpreter, with the general secretary
and deputy general secretary of the Patriotic Association. I also
met officials of the Protestant Three-Self Movement. While in
Hong Kong I had numerous conversations about China with
people of quite different background, competence and viewpoint.

For their part, members of the Patriotic Association make the
following points:

1. They state that no change of doctrine has taken place in the
Catholic Church in China.

2. They stress that responsibility for the present estrangement between Rome and themselves lies with Rome: by refusing
to approve their episcopal consecrations since 1958 the Vatican
showed no understanding of their extreme situation; by forbidding them to co-operate in any way with their government, the
Vatican forbade them, in effect, to love their country.

3. They are happy that the Vatican has now changed its mind
and allows Catholics to be patriotic. They go on to add, however,
that these words must now be followed by appropriate deeds.

4. They look forward to the normalisation of relations between themselves and the Pope and between the Vatican and
their government. They resent the Vatican's present diplomatic

relations with Taiwan, stressing that the Vatican is now the only state in Europe to recognise Taiwan.

5. They also resent the circulation in China of a Vatican document listing, in Latin and Chinese, various permissions granted by Rome to priests and faithful in China. They see this as divisive, as calling on the priests and people who are not members of the Patriotic Association to worship apart and in secret.

6. They are emphatic that the Catholic Church in China is not under government control. They explain that the church is ruled by the Episcopal Conference and the Church Affairs Committee; that the role of the Patriotic Association, membership of which is voluntary, is to act as a bridge between church and state, helping Catholics to be patriotic and to promote the four modernisations (agriculture, industry, defence, science and technology), and helping the government to know and understand the church's viewpoint.

Among those who are not members of the Patriotic Association a more sympathetic and nuanced attitude towards the Association and its members is now emerging. In my conversations the following points in particular struck me.

1. There is a new willingness to admit that in the past the church was too closely associated with the colonial powers and that (in the words of the late Bishop Francis Hsu of Hong Kong, which someone quoted for me from an address given in 1968), 'the church failed to make its message intelligible and obviously relevant', that it was 'a powerless, helpless spectator' in the 'phase of soul-searching agony' which China went through 'between the surge of rational, national renewal in 1919, and the Communist conquest of power in 1949'.

2. There is a new openness, a new readiness to listen to and to learn from the members of the Association. The mood is one, not of condemnation as before, but of understanding. As Pope John Paul II put it at Manila in February 1981:

> For many years we have not been able to have contact with each other ... But in those long years you have undoubtedly lived through other experiences which are still unknown, and at times you will have wondered in your consciences what was the right thing for you to do. For those who have never had such experiences it is difficult to appreciate fully such situations. (*Acta Apostolicae Sedis* 7;3 [1981] p 348.)

3. There is a new willingness to admit that, for all the Association's ambiguities, many of its members are good Catholics who have also suffered for the faith and who continue to believe at heart in the importance of communion with the Pope.

4. Whereas it was quite usual previously to refer to the Patriotic priests and people as 'the Patriotic Church' and to pray, at Benediction for instance, 'for those who have joined the Patriotic Church but who now repent and seek the way back to the fold', there is now a new sensitivity to the implications of this terminology as promoting schismatic attitudes and actions and a new determination to avoid it altogether.

5. There is a more sophisticated theology of the papacy and a new realisation that ecclesiastical 'self-government, self-support, self-propagation' ('independence, autonomy and self-rule') is not incompatible with papal primacy and full communion with the Holy See.

It only remains to add that those who were beginning to be more open in their attitude to the Patriotic Association and its members are growing in number, though they still have questions, especially about the government's role in church affairs and about the Association's analysis and interpretation of events. Pope John Paul, in a special message on 3 December 1996 to the bishops of China, addressed them according to Vatican II terminology as 'vicars and ambassadors of Christ', thereby reminding the Chinese political authorities that the bishops were not the Pope's 'vicars and ambassadors'. The Pope urged the bishops to recognise that they 'are called today, in a particular way, to express and promote full reconciliation between all the faithful'.

Quite clearly the situation and condition of the Catholic Church in China have changed considerably since I visited there in 1981. Then, for altogether understandable reasons, because it was just emerging from the isolation of the old Communist era, the church for the most part was pre-Vatican II in spirit and style. Now the Second Vatican Council has really arrived. Latin is much less the language of the liturgy. Despite periodical difficulties at regional or local levels, church life – the instruction and baptism of adults, the training of seminarians – continues and develops. The Vatican has a Cultural Office located in Hong

Kong but much broader in its interests and concerns. In charge of this Office at present is a Counsellor of the Vatican Nunciature in the Philippines and he happens to be an Irishman from Co Clare, Monsignor Eugene Nugent. A growing number of the bishops who are members of the Patriotic Association have secretly established communion with Rome, have had their episcopal consecrations validated by Rome. The number is variously put at 'the majority', 'between a half and two-thirds', 'all but eight'. However, the creation of this third category of bishop – those recognised both by Rome and by the government – only adds to the confusion of some Catholics, especially those who suffered persecution in the past.

But while the situation of the Catholic Church in China may now be more relaxed, alarm bells have begun to ring in Hong Kong about impending legislation which may curb the freedoms it enjoyed under British Rule and since 1997. The Catholic Bishop, Joseph Zen Ze-kiun, is leading the opposition and seems no longer as optimistic as he previously was about the future of the church in Hong Kong and in China (cf *The Tablet*, 4 January 2003, pp 6-7; *China Church News*, May 1997 p 9).

CHAPTER TEN

Ecumenism: Forty Years in the Desert?[1]

Ecumenism of course is now in its 90s, not in its 40s. It began in 1910 in Edinburgh at a meeting of the International Missionary Council. It is Catholic involvement in ecumenism which is in its 40s, but the birth of Catholic ecumenism in the 1960s meant a re-birth for Anglican, Orthodox and Protestant ecumenism. The 60s were a climacteric in the ecumenical movement in general. The winds of change were blowing strongly not only in the secular world but also in the whole Christian world.

In any case it remains that for Catholics at least ecumenism is now in its 40s and that the significance of this fact merits some consideration. Vatican II took place from 1962-1965. The Council's *Decree on Ecumenism* was promulgated on 21 November 1964 and was welcomed on all sides as 'revolutionary', 'epoch-making', 'a remarkable achievement, far surpassing what even the "ecumenical romantics" would have anticipated'. It was on Whit Sunday 1960 that Pope John XXIII had announced the establishment of what was initially called the Secretariat – now the Pontifical Council – for Promoting Christian Unity. Thanks to this body and its moderator, Cardinal Bea, almost all the other churches became involved in the Vatican Council by sending delegate observers. Later that same year, on 3 December, Archbishop Fisher of Canterbury, an Evangelical Anglican who had no great sympathy for Rome, called on the Pope at the Vatican and his first words were: 'Your Holiness, we are making history.' It was in fact the first visit of an Archbishop of

---

1. This is the text, somewhat modified, of a paper which was read at the International Congress of the Ecumenical Society of the Blessed Virgin Mary held at St Patrick's College, Maynooth in June 2001 and which was printed in Mary for *Earth and Heaven: Essays on Mary and Ecumenism*, eds William McLoughlin & Jill Pinnock, Gracewing, Leominster, 2002, pp 209-218.

Canterbury to the Pope since that of Archbishop Arundel in 1397. One immediate result was the appointment of a representative of the Archbishops of Canterbury and York to take up residence in Rome and the eventual establishment there of what is now the Anglican Centre.

Then no sooner had Vatican II ended in December 1965 than Pope Paul VI was off to Jerusalem where he and Archbishop Athenagoras, Patriarch of Constantinople, met and in what they called an 'act of justice and forgiveness' solemnly consigned to oblivion the excommunications of 1054. In March of the following year, 1966, Archbishop Michael Ramsey, Archbishop of Canterbury, was visiting Rome and receiving as a gift from the Pope his very own episcopal ring: a gesture richly if ambiguously symbolic in significance.[2] Soon afterwards the Anglican/Roman Catholic Joint Preparatory Commission was established. This was quickly followed by bilateral Commissions with the other churches, especially the Lutheran and Methodist – I myself was involved in the Methodist/Roman Catholic International Commission. And as early as 1968 the first fruits of this work began to appear. That year the Catholic Church became a full member of the Faith and Order Commission of the World Council of Churches and that year the Anglican/Roman Catholic Joint Preparatory Commission produced its 'Malta Report' which urged a strategy of unity by stages. Already, however, the first signs of difficulties to come had made their ominous appearance. The Congregation for the Doctrine of the Faith would not agree to the publication of the Malta Report.[3]

2. According to Owen Chadwick, in his *Michael Ramsey: A Life* (Oxford 1990, p 322), 'No Pope could have said anything louder about that vexing sore over the validity of Anglican Orders. It spoke more loudly than any bull or encyclical.' He goes on (ibid) to quote Ramsey himself stating at a press conference that 'What it does betoken is the official recognition of the Church of England as an official church with its rightful ministers. That from Rome means a great deal.' On the occasion of his 1989 visit to Rome, Archbishop Runcie referred to the ring as 'a sign not unlike an engagement ring'-- a token of commitment to fuller unity; cf Adrian Hastings, *Robert Runcie*, (London 1991, p 123.)

3. William Purdy, *The Search for Unity*, (London 1996, pp 112-114,121-123.) Copies of the Report were distributed to the Bishops of the Lambeth Conference during the Summer and eventually on 31 November the text was published in *The Tablet*.

For me the question now arises: has it any significance that it is forty years ago that all this happened? Sometimes, both in biblical and secular usage ,the figure 'forty' may indicate little more than a round number: the length of David's reign of forty years (2 Sam 5:4), the depth of 'the 40 foot' at high tide in Dúnlaoire, the number of Ali Baba's Forty Thieves. At other times, however, the meaning of forty in the bible is quite definitely much more than merely mathematical. It is hardly a coincidence that the Flood lasted forty days, that Israel wandered in the desert for forty years, that Jesus too spent forty days in the desert and forty hours in the tomb and remained on earth forty days after his resurrection and that our Lent lasts for forty days.

For the Christian, therefore, the figure 'forty' suggests a mysterious, fateful period. But if salvation history, as we have just seen, consists of such periods of forty, the central, fundamental one is Israel's wandering in the desert which the Book of Deuteronomy (8:2) describes so beautifully:

And you shall remember all the way which the Lord your God has led you these forty years in the wilderness, that he might humble you, testing you to know what was in your hearts, whether you would keep his commandments, or not.

The synoptic account of Jesus's forty days in the desert – especially that of Matthew and Luke culminating in the triple temptation – is generally accepted as a deliberate reference to Israel's desert experience. The desert is a place of danger, hardship and death, the haunt of demons and wild animals, a place to wrestle with evil, eventually to be saved, of course,[4] but primarily to be tempted and tested and, as the New Testament reminds us more than once (e.g. Acts 7:41, 1 Cor 10:5; Heb 3:8), to fail and be unfaithful, to drink the chalice of doubt and mistake, of failure and unfaithfulness.

Looking back now on the period since the 60s it makes sense

4. This note of hope, the assurance of salvation, is missing in the phrase 'the roaring forties'.This nautical phrase refers in general to 'stormy ocean tracts' and in particular to 'the exceptionally rough part of the Atlantic Ocean between 40 and 50 degrees North Latitude'. To speak of the ecumenical movement being in the roaring forties would, I think, merely suggest that it was having a stormy time, a stormy passage without holding out the hope of a safe passage and safe arrival.

to me to see it as a desert experience for the ecumenical movement and it reassures me, it gives me hope to realise that we are now in the last decade of this forty year period. These forty years have for ecumenists in particular been a period of ups and downs, of mistakes and failures, of disappointments, of trials and tribulations. It has been a period of probation. But the movement has grown in maturity.

These forty years of ecumenical endeavour have seen a heavy emphasis placed on doctrinal unity and on joint research and study as the privileged means of achieving this unity. The results have been quite remarkable. Agreed statements on the eucharist have been produced not only by the Anglican/Roman Catholic International Commission but by other bilateral commissions as well and indeed by the Faith and Order Commission of the World Council of Churches. The Pope has signed Common Christological Declarations with Eastern Patriarchs which seem to sit lightly to the teaching not only of the Council of Chalcedon but also of the Council of Ephesus. Rome no longer insists on a two-nature terminology nor on the term *theotokos*. As Pope John XXIII put it at the opening of Vatican II: 'the substance of the ancient doctrine of the deposit of faith is one thing, and the way in which it is presented is another'. And more recently a Joint Declaration on the Doctrine of Justification, the article on which the Lutherans see the church stand or fall, has been agreed by them and by the Roman Catholic Church. Unfortunately, Marian doctrine and devotion does not so far feature in this success story, despite all the good work of the Ecumenical Society of the BVM. The next Report of ARCIC will, however, be on Mary.

But this remarkably successful dialogue of truth has for all practical purposes remained a dead-letter. Addressing Patriarch Athenagoras in 1964, Pope Paul VI had stated:

Divergences of a doctrinal, liturgical and disciplinary nature will have to be examined, at the proper time and place, in a spirit of fidelity to truth and of understanding in charity. What can and must now begin to develop is that fraternal charity which is ingenious in discovering new ways of showing itself; which, taking its lessons from the past, is ready to pardon, more ready to believe good than evil.

In general, however, it is the doctrinal divergences between the churches which since the 1960s have received attention and indeed showed themselves amazingly amenable to solution. No comparable dialogue of charity, of joint action has developed either in parallel to the dialogue of truth or in consequence of its conclusions. The boldness which has characterised the churches' thinking has been conspicuously absent from their ways of acting. The 'co-operation among all Christians' to which Vatican II's *Decree on Ecumenism* had exhorted Roman Catholics, in its longest and most eloquent paragraph, has not for the most part become the norm but only the exception.

We do not in fact relate to each other or treat each other as sisters and, to that extent, recent Vatican documents simply exposed the hollowness of our ecumenism. It is our deeds rather than our words which express our real feelings and opinions about each other, our deeds in the matter for instance of integrated education/joint schooling, and in the matter of eucharistic sharing. From our deeds rather than words what emerges is, sadly, that we Christians have not yet fallen back in love with each other, that we have not yet abandoned the culture of contempt which makes us suspect and doubt each other's faith.

But as we enter the last decade of our forty years of wandering in the ecumenical desert, I discern one sign of a new maturity in interchurch relations: there is a change of vocabulary, of terminology, a changed theological emphasis. Whereas in earlier years we spoke in terms of unity and renewal, now we prefer to think and talk in the related but distinct terms of reconciliation, of repentance and forgiveness. Reconciliation is a term which in recent years has become very popular in secular as well as religious discourse. And so it comes as a surprise to find that there are very few – only five or six it would appear – references to 'reconciliation' in the whole corpus of Vatican II. The change of vocabulary, the new emphasis on reconciliation instead of unity is, I suggest, highly significant: it implies a distinction with a real difference. What is merely implicit in the language of unity and renewal becomes explicit in the language of reconciliation, of forgiveness and repentance. Here in this latter there is formal recognition of the following highly relevant facts: that it is groups of people, not sets of doctrinal or theological propositions, communities of belief rather than systems of belief, which primarily need to be brought into agreement; that the disunity to be overcome among Christians is a disunity of estrangement and alienation; that down the years we have hurt and offended each other and discriminated against each other and that, if this does not still continue, the memory of it does; that we have so far never really forgiven each other; that we harbour bitter memories, doubts and suspicions about each other; that if these lie hidden for the most part, they surface only too clearly in resistance to Agreed Statements, in various forms of sectarianism, not excluding violence, in general ecumenical apathy, in the ungenerous provisions of *One Bread One Body*, and in the clumsy insensitivities of the Vatican Declaration *Dominus Jesus* and its Note on 'Sister Churches'.

But where there has been hurt and offence, renewal in a relationship must take the form of forgiveness and repentance, and unity must take the form of reconciliation. The unity which is reconciliation, whether it be the reconciliation of two individuals or two groups or two societies either secular or religious, makes demands on both victims and offenders. Faults, however, are rarely if ever all on one side. Each of us, therefore, is very likely both victim and offender so that it is mutual forgiveness and mutual repentance which are in order. In any case if there is to be reconciliation it is necessary that the victims forgive: that they abandon thoughts of revenge or retribution; that they persevere in love for the offenders but paradoxically without in any way condoning the offence. And certainly if there is to be reconciliation it is also necessary that the offenders repent, i.e. that they confess, apologise, say sorry and give concrete expression to these words of sorrow by making amends, by undoing the wrong committed, making compensation, restoring justice .

But all this is very complex and still quite controversial. There are some who reject the concept of reconciliation because it seems to them to softpedal, to downplay if not ignore the claims of justice/repentance, or who accept it with a one-sided emphasis on justice/repentance, softpedalling the claims of forgiveness. These differences surfaced in the context of the Jubilee Year. In his 1994 Apostolic Letter on 'Preparation for the Jubilee of the Year 2000', Pope John Paul emphasised that the church

cannot cross the threshold of the new millennium without
encouraging her children to purify themselves, through repentance of past errors and instances of infidelity, inconsist-
ency, and slowness to act. (#33)

After six years of research into the church's record of past errors,
the Pope on Sunday 12 March celebrated a Jubilee Day of
Pardon. Each of seven leading figures of the Roman Curia con-
fessed in turn 'sins committed in the service of the truth', 'sins
which have harmed the unity of the Body of Christ', 'sins
against the people of Israel', 'sins committed in actions against
love, peace, the rights of peoples and respect for cultures and religions', 'sins against the dignity of women and the unity of the
human race', and 'sins in relation to the fundamental rights of
the human person'. In each case the Pope asked for forgiveness.
At the beginning he had mentioned 'the wrongs done by others
to us', to the Christians who had 'suffered injustices, arrogance
and persecution for their faith', urging a renewed offer of forgiveness in order 'to purify the memory of those sad events from
every sentiment of rancour or revenge'.

This Day of Pardon was a deeply moving occasion but, as
mentioned, the prospect had given rise to a good deal of misgiv-
ing among some theologians and historians. To address these
misgivings the Pope had asked the International Theological
Commission to study the issue. Their report, in the drafting of
which Rev Professor Tom Norris of Maynooth had taken part,
was published earlier in the month. Entitled *Memory and
Reconciliation: The Church and the Faults of the Past*, this document
discusses the problems arising and by way of answer emphasises the 'solidarity that exists among them [the children of the
church] through time and space because of their incorporation
into Christ and the work of the Holy Spirit'. (3.4) In other words
the principles of logic and theology which enable us to pride
ourselves on our past and its glories, these same principles enable and require us to be ashamed about, to ask forgiveness for,
to do penance for what is inglorious and sinful in that same past,
for the evils which our ancestors perpetrated; and also of course
to offer forgiveness for the evils suffered by those ancestors, to
offer it to those who are and who recognise themselves as the
heirs and successors of the perpetrators.

Here in Ireland in a 1996 letter our Catholic bishops had stated: 'We must all respond generously to the Pope's call to the whole church for a collective examination of conscience regarding the mistakes and sins of this millennium, especially sins against Christian unity.' And the following year a report of the Department of Theological Questions of the Irish InterChurch meeting (an association of all the churches, Catholic and Protestant) recommended, among other things, that the churches come together in a common confession of guilt, and a common desire for reconciliation, in Ireland North and South. In that spirit the Anglican and Catholic Bishops of Ferns, Bishop Brendan Comiskey and Bishop John Neill, did issue a Joint Pastoral Letter for Pilgrimage Sunday, 21 May 2000. In this letter they recalled how 'relationships between us as churches have undergone a sea-change' and added:

> Grateful as we are for that flowering of ecumenical fellowship, goodwill and co-operation, we cannot but feel called to ask God's and each other's forgiveness for the many divisive, wounding and unChristian attitudes, policies and practices that found their way into both our churches during the centuries since the Reformation. We each express true repentance on behalf of our own church for these hurtful and damaging words and deeds, and we pray that the reconciliation all of us in both churches seek may be brought nearer by our request for forgiveness and our expression of true conversion of heart in relation to these ecumenical faults and failings.

The Catholic Archbishop of Dublin and other individual Catholic bishops did during the Jubilee year emphasise forgiveness and reconciliation, but mainly with particular reference to recent scandals rather than in the comprehensive way adopted by the Pope. The Jubilee Day of Pardon which the Pope celebrated in Rome on 12 March went unobserved here. And as a body the Irish Catholic bishops seem to have no plans to follow the Pope's example in this matter. Many Catholics of course disapprove of this papal initiative. When in 1997 Bishop Walsh of Killaloe asked forgiveness from Protestants for the 'pain and hurt' caused by the *Ne Temere* decree and mixed marriages in the past, his gesture was dismissed in articles in the *Irish Catholic* and in an editorial in the *Catholic Herald* (17 May 1997) as 'cultural

cringe' and 'misleading digression'. With reference however to
our neglect of the Day of Pardon the editor of the Irish Catholic ,
David Quinn, wrote as follows in his *Sunday Times* column on 19
March:

> Let down by the usual failure of imagination, nothing was
> forthcoming from the Irish hierarchy, apart from Dublin's
> Archbishop Desmond Connell. The Irish bishops, collectively
> could have done something dramatic last Sunday [12 March]
> for all the wrongs committed in the name of the Irish church.
> It might even have convinced some people and won back lost
> ground. Instead they did nothing. Another opportunity lost.

While the change of terminology and of theology from unity to
reconciliation is a sign of maturity, resistance to it is also a sign
that we are still wandering in the desert. In particular, this re-
sistence highlights the fact that we have paid too little attention
to the dialogue of charity, that this has suffered by contrast with
the dialogue of truth. This resistance therefore invites and chal-
lenges us to begin at last to follow the advice of Paul VI in 1964
when addressing Patriach Athenagoras:

> What can and must now begin to develop is that fraternal
> charity which is ingenious in discovering new ways of show-
> ing itself, which, taking its lessons from the past, is ready to
> pardon, more ready to believe good than evil.

The same advice is given by Pope John Paul II when in his
Apostolic Letter, *At the Beginning of the New Millennium*, he urges
us 'to launch out into the deep' (Luke 5:4). This must mean aban-
doning our fears, of joint schools for instance and of eucharistic
sharing, and taking seriously the call to co-operation according
to conscience in paragraph 12 of the *Decree on Ecumenism*. In the
words of the Decree, 'Through such co-operation, all believers in
Christ are able to learn easily how they can understand each
other better and esteem each other more, and how the road to
the unity of Christians may be made smooth.' Such co-operation,
doing everything together as far as conscience permits, has been
the ecumenical ideal since the Faith and Order Conference in
Lund in 1952. The churches in Europe in their recent *Charta
Oecumenica* have formally committed themselves to such co-
operation : 'We commit ourselves to act together at all levels of
church life wherever conditions permit and there are no reasons

of faith or overriding expediency mitigating against this'. And the promotion of such co-operation seems to be the main concern of the new International Anglican/Roman Catholic Commission For Unity and Mission (IARCCUM) which first met in London and Rome in November 2001 and in Malta from 19-23 November 2002.

In any case, despite this resistance, an ecumenical journey in the desert, a desert experience of forty years for the ecumenical movement, is not a cause for doom and gloom. At the end must lie the promised land. So I look forward to the next decade and it begins, I note, very promisingly and very providentially in its very first year, in 2010 with the centenary of Edinburgh 1910 and continues in 2014 equally promisingly and providentially with the Golden Jubilee of the promulgation of Vatican II's *Decree on Ecumenism*, in 1964. These past forty years of ecumenism have indeed been a time of trial, of temptation, a time of too much inept leadership and too many botched initiatives; they still are. But against the background of biblical salvation history it is, in the words of Moses in Deut 8:2, the Lord our God who is leading us during these forty years in the ecumenical wilderness. It has been a learning experience; we have grown in ecumenical maturity. We believe that as a people we will get to the promised land of Christian unity. And we know that we shall get there, not by the methods used by Joshua, not by conquest and conversions and not by a dialogue of truth alone, but by a dialogue of truth and a dialogue of charity in proper combination. We do not yet know what the promised land of Christian unity will really be like. At times, like Moses and like Martin Luther King, we've been to the mountain top; we've looked over and seen the promised land, a land overflowing with milk and honey; with the milk and honey of human kindness, of Christian charity, of mutual forgiveness and repentance, of reconciliation, with shared pulpits and shared eucharists. So we travel 'buoyed up by hope' (Rom 12:12) with the hope that does not disappoint (Rom 5:5) but still accepting that while we wander in the desert to hope is to hope against hope. (cf Rom 4:18.)

Michael Hurley SJ
A Bibliography[1]

1948

1 'Francisco Suárez SJ (1548-1948)', *Irish Monthly* 76 (1948), pp 265-73

2 'The Communist Manifesto 1848-1948', *Irish Monthly* 76 (1948), pp 532-40

1951

3 'Illumination according to S. Bonaventure', *Gregorianum* 32 (1951), pp 388-404

1953

4 'Belgian Workers Today', *Social Order* 3 (1953), pp 109-16

5 'The Belgian Enterprise Councils, 1948-53', *The American Catholic Sociological Review* 14 (1953), pp 218-29

1960

6 'Scriptura Sola: Wyclif and his Critics', *Traditio* 16 (1960), pp 275-352

7 'Scriptura Sola: Wicleffus ejusque Interpretes', *Verbum Domini* 38 (1960), pp 223-9

1961

8 *Towards Christian Unity: An Introduction to the Ecumenical Movement* (Dublin, 1961), pp 36

9 'Feast of the Ascension: The Mystery and Its Significance', *The Irish Ecclesiastical Record* 95 (1961), pp 255-62

10 'Born Incorruptibly: The Third Canon of the Lateran Council (AD 649)', *The Heythrop Journal* 2 (1961), pp 216-36

11 'The New Delhi Programme of the World Council of Churches I', *The Irish Theological Quarterly* 28 (1961), pp 303-17

12 'Christian Unity', *Doctrine and Life* 11 (1961), pp 532-42

13 'The World Council of Churches and its Forthcoming Assembly', *Studies* 50 (1961), pp 327-42

---

1. This is a revised and updated version of the Bibliography printed in *Reconciliation: Essays in Honour of Michael Hurley*, ed. Oliver Rafferty SJ, Dublin, The Columba Press, 1993 pp 293-301.

1962

14 'The Ascension of Our Lord: The Mystery and its Significance',
    Sermons for Sundays and Feasts, ed P. J. Hamell, (Dublin 1962), pp
    215-22 (Reprint of No 9)

15 'The New Delhi Programme of the World Council of Churches II',
    The Irish Theological Quarterly 29 (1962), pp 52-67

16 'The Vatican Council: The Issues and the Intention', *The Irish Times*
    23 January 1962, p 7

17 'Some Recent Ecumenical Literature', *The Irish Theological Quarterly*
    29 (1962), pp 248-58

18 'The Vatican Council and the Ecumenical Situation Today', *The Irish
    Ecclesiastical Record* 98 (1962), pp 28-42

19 'The World Council of Churches' Recent Paris Meeting', *The Irish
    Times* 3, 4 September 1962

1963

20 (ed.) *Praying for Unity. A Handbook of Studies, Meditations and Prayers*
    (The Furrow Trust 1963), pp 240. Editor's Introduction, pp 24-31

21 'Catholics and the Council', *Praying for Unity* (= No 20), pp 104-16

22 'The Nature of the Church: Common Ground between Catholics
    and Protestants', *Doctrine and Life* 13 (1963), pp 15-25

23 'An Octave of Prayer', *The Furrow* 14 (1963), pp 49-54

24 'Common Ground between Catholics and Protestants' *Guide* (New
    York) 178 (May 1963), pp 8-13 (Reprint of No 22)

25 'Ecumenism and Mariology: The Contribution of Catholics' *The
    Furrow* 14 (1963), pp 212-24

26 'Ecumenism and Mariology: The Contribution of Protestants', *The
    Furrow* 14 (1963), pp 349-60

27 'The Montreal Ecumenical Conference', *The Irish Press* 13 July 1973,
    p 8

28 'The Second Vatican Council', *Biblical Theology* 13 (Oct 1963), pp 52-9

29 'A Pre-Tridentine Theology of Tradition. Thomas Netter of Walden
    (+1430)', *The Heythrop Journal* 4 (1963), pp 348-66

30 'Praying for the Catholic Church', *The Clergy Review* 48 (1963), pp
    739-50 (=Reprint of No 21)

1964

31 'Ecumenism and Conversion', *The Irish Theological Quarterly* 31 (1964), pp 132-49

32 'Presbyterians in Council. The Reformed Churches Four Hundred Years After', *Studies* 53 (1964), pp 286-304

33 'Hoping with Hope. The Vatican Council's Decree on Ecumenism', *The Irish Times* 30 November 1964, p 6

1965

34 'Presbyterians in Council. The Reformed Churches Four Hundred Years After', *Biblical Theology* 15 (March 1965), pp 1-14 (=Reprint of No 32)

35 'Conditional Baptism', *The Furrow* 16 (1965), pp 87-92

36 'Joint Worship', *The Furrow* 16 (1965), pp 233-9

37 'The Five Per Cent', *The Furrow* 16 (1965), pp 370-4

38 'Presbyterians and Repentance', *The Furrow* 16 (1965), pp 493-5

39 'The Churches' Industrial Council', *The Furrow* 16 (1965), pp 625-8

40 'Non-Sectarianism or Christian Co-operation?', *The Furrow* 16 (1965), pp 770-2

1966

41 (ed.) *Church and Eucharist*, (Dublin and Melbourne 1966), pp 298. Editor's Introduction, pp 11-27

42 'The Church in Protestant Theology. Some Reflections on the Fourth Book of Calvin's Institutes', *The Meaning of the Church* [Papers of the Maynooth Union Summer School 1965] (Dublin and Melbourne 1966) pp 110-43

43 'The Ecumenism Decree: Facts and Reflections', *The Irish Ecclesiastical Record* 105 (1966), pp 12-26

44 'The Greenhills Conference', *The Furrow* 17 (1966), pp 124-7

45 'Dialogue at Local Level', *The Furrow* 17 (1966), pp 246-8

46 'Mixed Marriages', *The Furrow* 17 (1966), pp 279-87

47 'The Third Glenstal Ecumenical Conference', *The Furrow* 17 (1966), pp 517-9

48 'Clerical Students' Convention', *The Furrow* 17 (1966), pp 649-51

49 'The Church in Protestant Theology. Some Reflections on the Fourth Book of Calvin's Institutes', *Biblical Theology* 16 (October 1966), pp 1-15 (=Reprint of No 42)

50 'Non Anglicani sed Angli?', *The Furrow* 17 (1966), pp 781-6

51 'The Message of World Methodism', *The Irish Times* 29 August 1966

1967

52 'Penance: Sacrament of Reconciliation', *Sin and Repentance* [Papers of the Maynooth Union Summer School 1966], ed. Denis O'Callaghan, (Dublin and Sydney 1967), pp 109-26

53 Penance: Sacrament of Reconciliation', *The Furrow* 18 (1967), pp 67-80 (=Reprint of No 52)

54 'What can Catholics learn from the Infant Baptism Controversy?' *Concilium* 4 (April 1967), pp 9-12. (='The Sacraments. An Ecumenical Dilemma' *Concilium* Vol 24, ed. Hans Kung, (New York 1967), pp 16-23

55 'The Ecumenical Spirit', *The Capuchin Annual* 34 (1967), pp 251-8

56 'The Problem of Original Sin', *The Clergy Review* 52 (1967), pp 770-86

1968

57 (ed.) *Ecumenical Studies: Baptism and Marriage* (Dublin 1968), pp 240. Editor's Preface, pp 9-22

58 (ed.) *John Wesley's Letter to a Roman Catholic* (London-Belfast 1968), pp 64. Editor's Preface, pp 7-10; Introduction, pp 22-47

59 'The Problem of Baptism', *Ecumenical Studies: Baptism and Marriage*, pp 23-60 (= No 57)

60 'Christ and Divorce', *Ecumenical Studies: Baptism and Marriage*, pp 220-40 (= No 57)

60a 'Christ and Divorce', *Irish Theological Quarterly* 35 (1968), pp 58-72 (Reprint of No 60)

61 'Mixed Marriages: The Canonical Form', *The Furrow* 19 (1968), pp 94-7 (=extract from Editor's Preface in No 57)

62 (ed.) *John Wesley's Brev Till en Romersk Katolik*, Nya Bokforlags Aktiebolaget, Stockholm, 1968, pp 72 (=Swedish translation of No 58)

63 'Church and World', *The Capuchin Annual* 35 (1968), pp 107-20

64 'Belief and Trust', *Doctrine and Life* 18 (1968), pp 461-4

1969

65 *Theology of Ecumenism* [Theology Today No 9], Cork, 1969, pp 96

66 'Mixed Marriages: The Lund Principle', *One in Christ*, 5(1969),
    pp 96-102.

67 'George Tyrrell: Some Post-Vatican II Impressions', *The Heythrop
    Journal* 10 (1969), pp 243-55

68 'The Sacrament of Unity: Intercommunion and some Forgotten
    Truths', *The Way* 9 (1969), pp 107-17

69 'The Practice of Ecumenism', *Hibernia* 31 January-13 February 1969,
    p 6

69a 'Ultimate Goal is Union', *Irish Independent* 26 September 1969, p 8

1970

70 Teologia dell' Ecumenismo (Catania, Edizioni Paolini, 1970), pp 135
    (=Italian Edition of No 64)

71 (ed.) *Irish Anglicanism 1869-1969* (Dublin 1970), pp xi + 236. Editor's
    Preface pp vii-xi

72 'The Future', *Irish Anglicanism 1869-1969* (= No 71), pp 211-27

73 'Bibliography on Ecumenism', *The Irish Theological Quarterly* 36 (1969),
    pp 327-52

74 'Ecumenism: What and Why?', *The Furrow* 21 (1970), pp 416-27

75 'Irish Ecumenism: Courtship to Engagement', *The Irish Press* 2
    February 1970, p 11

76 'Papal Power a Hundred Years After', *The Church of Ireland Magazine*
    (5 April 1970), pp 1-5

1971

77 *L'Oecumenisme* (Quebec 1971), pp 93 (French edition of No 65)

78 *Teologia del Ecumenismo* (Mexico, 1971), pp 127 (Spanish edition of
    No 65)

78a *Teologia dell' Ecumenismo* (Catania 1971), pp 133 (Italian edition of
    No 65)

79 'Christian Unity', *Intercom, A Bulletin of the Catholic Communications
    Institute of Ireland* January 1971, p 12

80 'The Irish School of Ecumenics', *One in Christ* 7 (1971), pp 66-9

81 'The Irish School of Ecumenics', *The Month* 3 (1971), pp 147-8

82 'Eucharistic Agreement', *The Sunday Press* 19 September 1971

1972

83 'The Irish School of Ecumenics', *The Capuchin Annual* 39 (1972), pp 77-80

84 'The Anglican-Roman Catholic Agreed Statement on Eucharistic Doctrine: A Comment', *The Furrow* 23 (1972), pp 23-6

1973

85 'Interchurch Marriage', *One in Christ* 9 (1973), pp 35-42

86 'Eucharist: Means and Expressions of Unity', *One in Christ* 9 (1973), pp 270-83

87 'Ecumenism and Common Worship', *One in Christ* 9 (1973), pp 354-63

88 'The Irish School of Ecumenics', *Intercom, A Bulletin of the Catholic Communications Institute of Ireland* September 1973, p 6

89 'First Impressions: from Canterbury to Jerusalem?', *The Irish Times* 13 December 1973, p 7

90 (ed.) 'Report on the International Consultation on Mixed Marriage, Dublin, 2-6 September 1974', *One in Christ* 11 (1975), pp 88-96; *The Furrow* 26 (1975), pp 126-31; *Doctrine and Life* 25 (1975), pp 156-64; *Theology* 78 (1975), pp 75-82

91 (ed.) *Beyond Tolerance: The Challenge of Mixed Marriage* (London 1975), pp xi + 193. Editor's Introduction, pp ix-xi

1976

92 'New Directory on Ecumenism', *The Furrow* 27 (1976), pp 491-3

93 'Salvation Today and Wesley Today', *The Place of Wesley in the Christian Tradition*, ed. Kenneth E. Rowe (Metuchen 1976), pp 94-116

1977

94 'Ireland's Ecumenics School', *The Word* January 1977, pp 11-14

1978

95 'Baptism in Ecumenical Perspective', *One in Christ* 14 (1978), pp 106-23

96 'Ecumenism, Ecumenical Theology and Ecumenics', *Irish Theological Quarterly* 45 (1978), pp 132-9

97 'Berkeley and Methodism: A New Letter', *Berkeley Newsletter*, Trinity College, Dublin No 2 (November 1978), pp 1-2

1979

98 'The Scandal of Disunity', *The Furrow* 30 (1979), pp 40-4

99 'Baptism in Ecumenical Perspective', *Foundations. A Baptist-Journal of Theology and History* 22 (1979), pp 218-32 (Reprint of No 95)

1980

100'A Decade of Ecumenism', *Doctrine and Life* 30 (1980), pp 21-7

101'Human Rights Within the Church', *The Furrow* 31 (1980), pp 44-6

1981

102'Christian Spring in China', *The Tablet*, 23 May 1981, pp 493-5

103'An Ecumenist on Mount Athos', *The Irish Times Weekend Supplement* January 1981, p 11

1983

103a 'Christian Unity by 2000?' *Tantur Yearbook*, pp 53-67 (= No 104)

104'Christian Unity by 2000?', *One in Christ* 19 (1983), pp 2-13

105'Two Decades of Ecumenism', *Doctrine and Life* (September 1983), pp 399-414

106'George Tyrrell: Some post-ARCIC Impressions', *One in Christ* 19/3 (1983), pp 250-4

1984

107 'Peace-Making in Lent', *Doctrine and Life* (March 1984,) pp 132-6

108'Reconciliation in Northern Ireland: The Contribution of Ecumenism', *Studies* 73 (Winter 1984), pp 300-8

1985

109'20 Years after Vatican II: Ecumenism: Time for the Breakthrough', *The Month* (April 1985), pp 126-8

1986

110'The Eucharist in the Columbanus Community', *Religious Life Review* 25 (March-April 1986), pp 90-99

111'The Spirit of Forgiveness', *Pace* 18/1 (Spring 1986), pp 9-10

112'Ecumenism and Politics', *The Newman Review* (Spring 1986), pp 37-40

112a 'Ecumenical Sharing in Belfast', *The Ecumenical Review* 38/4 (October 1986), pp 378-380

1987

113 'Reconciliation in Northern Ireland', *The Furrow* 38 (January 1987), pp 9-16

114 'I Thirst: A Good Friday Meditation', *Religious Life Review* 26 (March-April 1987), pp 85-9

115 'Reconciliation in Northern Ireland: The Contribution of the Churches', *Reconciliation in Northern Ireland* [Papers of the Social Study Conference 1986], pp 69-78

116 'Northern Ireland: A Challenge to Theology', *Northern Ireland: A Challenge to Theology*, Centre for Theology and Public Issues, University of Edinburgh [Occasional Papers No 121], pp 20-8

1989

117 'Goings and Comings', *Search* 12/2 (Winter 1989), pp 53-7

1991

118 'Ecumenism: The Forgotten Dimensions', *The Month* (Sept-Oct 1991), pp 453-5

119 'Ecumenists: Missionaries with a Difference', *AMDG* 1991, pp 534

1992

120 'The Way Forward', *Pace* 24/1 (Summer 1992), pp 19-21

121 'Jesuits and the Protestants Today', *Studies* (Summer 1992), pp 203-11

122 'George Otto Simms (1910-1991)', *Studies* (Summer 1992), pp 212-6

123 'Trinity College Dublin 1592-1992: Reflections of a Jesuit Ecumenist', *Studies* (Winter 1992), pp 399-407

1994

124 'We had Hoped', *Doctrine and Life* (February 1994), pp 106-109

125 'The Beginnings of the Columbanus Community of Reconciliation', *One in Christ* (1994/1), pp 61-74

126 (ed.) *Reconciliation in Religion and Society* (Belfast 1994), pp xi +210. Editor's Introduction, pp 1-5

127 'Triple Vocation', *Call and Response*, ed. Frances Makower (London 1994), pp 135-147

128 'Gales of Change' [Book Review] *Studies* (Winter 1994), pp 466-468

1995

129 'In Retrospect – Irish Anglicanism', *Search* 18/1 (Spring 1995), pp 14-23

130 'Orthodox Visions of Ecumenism. On the Way to Fuller Koinonia' [Book Review] *Studies* (Spring 1995), pp 90-92

131 'Called to be Peacemakers', *The Sacred Heart Messenger* (August 1995), pp 2-5

132 'Forgiveness', *The Irish Times* 24 October 1995

133 'A Jesuit Thanks the Franciscans', *Religious Life Review* (September-October 1995), pp 283-288

134 'Jesuit Saint and Jesuit Prodigal', *Religious Life Review* (November-December 1995), pp 322-327

135 'Praying for Unity', *Intercom*, (December 1995-January 1996), pp 22-23

1996

136 'Forgiveness Forgotten?', *The Mustard Seed* (Washington DC, Jesuit Refugee Service/USA) Spring 1996, pp 16-17

137 'Further Studies and GC34', *EJIF Review* 8/2 (February 1996), pp 18-21

138 'An Ecumenical Mass – A Unity Week Afterthought', *The Furrow* 47/3 (March 1996), pp 152-156

139 'Hope and Forgiveness', *The Month* 29/6 (June 1996), pp 238-240

140 'To Earth from Heaven: A Christmas Sermon', *Intercom* 26/11 (December 1996-January 1997), p 37

141 'The Immaculate Conception', *Doctrine and Life* 46/10 (December 1996), pp 600-602

1997

142 'The Irish School of Ecumenics', *Jesuits* (January 1997), pp 75-6

143 'Reconciliation and the Churches in Northern Ireland', *The Reconciliation of Peoples Challenge to the Churches*, eds. Gregory Baum and Harold Wells, (Orbis Books 1997), pp 118-128

144 'The Message and Ministry of Reconciliation', *The Sacred Heart Messenger* (June 1997), pp 2-5

145 'Reconciliation and Forgiveness', *The Jurist* 56/1 (1996), pp 465-486

146 'Fr Kyran Fitzgerald SJ 1922-1997', *Interfuse* 92 (August 1997), pp 8-13

147 'Church Unity and World Peace', *Intercom* (December/January), p 42

148 'How the Irish School of Ecumenics Began', *One in Christ* 33/4 (Winter 1997), pp 298-316

1998

149 'Christian Unity by the Year 2000? – Part I', *Doctrine and Life* 48/1 (January 1998), pp 18-30

150 'Christian Unity by the Year 2000 – Part II', *Doctrine and Life* 48/2 (February 1998) pp 82-93

151 'Eucharistic Sharing', *The Furrow* 49/3 (March 1998), pp 143-149

152 'A Communion of Hope', *The Messenger*, April 1998, pp 2-5

153 'Ecumenism and Pentecost – From Despondency to Hope', *Reality* 63/5 (May 1998) pp 11-12

154 'Mary is for Everyone' [Book Review] *The Month*, May 1998, pp 202-203

155 'The Baptism of Johanna', *Spirituality*, Sept-Oct 1998, pp 287-289

156 'The Preparatory Years', *The Irish Inter-Church Meeting: Background and Development* (Belfast: Irish Inter-Church Meeting, 1998) pp 3-39

157 *Christian Unity: An Ecumenical Second Spring?*, (Dublin, Veritas 1998), pp xvi + 420

158 'Celebrating 25 Years of Ballymascanlon', *The Irish Times* 29 September 1998; *Church of Ireland Gazette* 16 October, p 12

159 'Hope and the Quest for Christian Unity', *Doctrine and Life* 48/9 (November 1998), pp 542-546

160 'Unity and Holiness: The Una Sancta', *Search* 21/2 (Winter 1998), pp 106-109

1999

161 'When the Powers Fall', *The Month* (March 1999), pp 116-117 [Book Review]

162 'One Bread, One Body' [Review Article] *Studies* 88 (Summer 1999) pp 225-230

163 'In Memoriam Henry Robert McAdoo', *Doctrine and Life* 49/6 (July/August 1999) pp 350-355

164 'Special Day for Catholics and Lutherans', *The Irish Times* 26 October 1999, p 14

165'If You Hear My Voice', *The Sacred Heart Messenger* (December 1999), pp 4-7

166'The new millennium: an ecumenical second spring?' *One in Christ* 35/3 (1999), pp 199-217

167'Occasional Eucharistic Sharing', *Religious Life Review* 38 (November-December 1999), pp 365-368

168'Ecumenism: Responding from the Viewpoint of an Active European Ecumenist', *Review of Ignatian Spirituality* 30/3 (1999), pp 89-92

169'Together on the Way' [Book Review], *Studies* 88 (Winter 1999) pp 464-466

2000

170'Ecumenism and the 20th Century', *Religious Life Review* 39 (January-February 2000) pp 38-45

171'Eric Gallagher: Peacemaker', *Doctrine and Life* 50/2 (February 2000) pp 87-90

172'The Joint Declaration on Justification: Another Ecumenical Milestone?' *Milltown Studies* 45 (Summer 2000) pp 44-57

173'The Lutheran-Catholic Joint Declaration: Another Ecumenical Milestone', *One in Christ* 36/1 (2000) pp 3-6

174 'Secolarismo e Liberta Religiosa: Religious Liberty and Secularism' [Book Review], *The Month* (May 2000), pp 202-203

175'Pentecost and Renewal', *Doctrine and Life* 50/5 (May-June 2000) pp 258-265

176'The Presbyterian Church in Ireland' [Book Review], *Studies* (Summer 2000), pp 184-187

177'The Enigmatic Malachi Martin', *Interfuse* (Spring/Summer 2000), pp 18-23

178'A Time to Build' [Book Review], *Search* 23/1 (Spring 2000), pp 81-85

179'Tetchiness returns to inter-church relations', *The Irish Times* 12 September 2000, p 14

180'Father Billy Kelly SJ', *Interfuse* (2000), No 105, pp 51-56

181'Ecumenical Hopes for the New Millennium', *Studies* 89/356 (Winter 2000), pp 364-369

2001

182'Ecumenism and Mariology', *One in Christ* 36/4 (Winter 2000) pp 296-316

183 'Irish School of Ecumenics: A Red-letter Day', *Religious Life Review* 40 (March-April 2001) pp 110-115

184 'Irish School of Ecumenics and Trinity College Dublin: Thirty Years a-Growing', *Interfuse* (Winter/Spring 2001), pp 3-8

185 'L'Irlanda del Nord e le Chiese dopo il Vaticano II: le difficolta di un cammino ecumenico', *Storia religiosa dell'Irlanda* (Milan: Centro Ambrosiano 2001), pp 447-470

186 'Week of Prayer for Christian Unity', *The Furrow* 52/3 (March 2001) pp 174-175

187 'Hopes for the New Millennium', *Hopes for the New Millennium* (St Patrick's Cathedral Publications 2001), pp 9-15

188 'Reconciliation: A Meditation on St Luke', *Doctrine and Life* 51/6 (July-August 2001), pp 356-361

189 'A Jesuit Agenda', *Interfuse* (Summer/Autumn 2001) No 109, pp 2-10

190 'A Jesuit Agenda: Reconciling Justice and Forgiveness', *National Jesuit News* (Washington DC) 31/3 (December 2001) pp 10-11, 19 (reprint of 189)

2002

191 'A Search for Peace', *The Sacred Heart Messenger* (June 2002), pp 4-7

192 'Not of this World' [Book Review], *Irish Theological Quarterly*, 87/1 (Spring 2002), pp 87-9

193 'Ecumenism and Mariology Today', *Mary for Earth and Heaven* (Gracewing 2002), pp 185-208 (cf 182)

194 'Interchurch Relations: Forty Years in the Desert?', *Mary for Earth and Heaven* (Gracewing 2002), pp 209-218

195 'Northern Ireland and the post-Vatican II ecumenical journey', *Christianity in Ireland: Revisiting the Story*, eds. Brendan Bradshaw and Daire Keogh (Dublin, The Columba Press, 2002), pp 259-270 (cf 185)

196 'Forgiveness/Mercy as well as Justice?', *Interfuse* 113 (Autumn 2002), pp 37-39

197 'East-West Interchurch Relations in Europe: The Ecumenical Methodology of Forgiveness', *Acta, Consultation [on] The Role of Jesuits in Catholic-Orthodox Relations in Europe: Past, Present, Future, Velehrad 2002*, (Rome, [Jesuit] Secretariat for Interreligious Dialogue, 2002), pp 80-100

198'Jesuit Agenda for Renewal', *JCTR Jesuit Supplement*, (November 2002, Lusaka, Jesuit Centre for Theological Reflection), pp 12-15 [Reprint of 189]

199'Europe: breathing with both lungs and sharing its gifts', *National Jesuit News*, Washington DC, (February-March 2003), p 7